POKER
ALICE TUBBS
The Straight Story

POKER ALICE TUBBS

The Straight Story

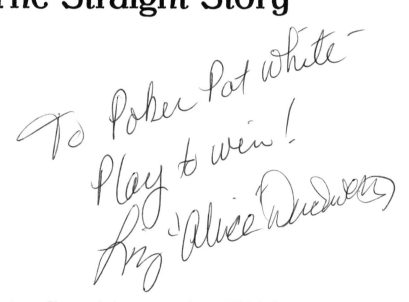

To Poker Pot White —
Play to win !
Liz "Alice Duckworth"

A Lady Gambler in the Wild West

by Liz Morton Duckworth

FILTER PRESS, LLC
Palmer Lake, Colorado

ISBN: 978-0-86541-253-8
Library of Congress Control Number: 2018948924

Front cover image used courtesy South Dakota State Historical Society, South Dakota Digital Archives (2008—07-07-035)

Back cover portrait of Alice Tubbs used courtesy Deadwood History, Inc., Adams Museum Collection, Deadwood, SD

Cover & Interior design by Robert Schram, Bookends Design

Published by Filter Press, LLC, Palmer Lake, CO 80133

Manufactured in the United States of America

Dedication

*To Women Writing the West, an outstanding organization
that promotes the contributions made by women to the history,
culture, and growth of the American West. Their leaders, members,
and resources have inspired me for many years.*

Contents

Acknowledgments

♠ MY THANKS to the wonderful team at Deadwood History, Inc. and the Homestake Adams Research and Cultural Center, especially Rachel, Rose, and Jenna.

Deepest appreciation to Jan Jacobs and other dedicated volunteers at the Creede Historical Society, and to Johanna for including my Poker Alice performances in many fundraising programs.

Thanks to the knowledgeable and helpful staff members at the South Dakota Historical Society, South Dakota Digital Archives, Denver Public Library, Western History Collection, History Colorado, Lake County Public Library, Colorado Mountain History, and Penrose Library Special Collections.

I am especially grateful to Linda Hasselstrom for her insights, editorial guidance, and a special place to work and study, Windbreak House Writing Retreat at Homestead House.

I am so grateful to my friend, Janis, who managed to get her hands on the 1987 classic film, *Poker Alice,* so we could watch it together and comment on wardrobe and hairstyle choices.

Thanks to Jane Ambrose Morton—my mom—who traveled with me to Deadwood and Sturgis, and to my dad, Richard J. Morton, for encouraging me to come to Creede and share its history.

The Ghost of Poker Alice

♠ THE GHOST OF POKER ALICE TUBBS nudged me one summer day in Creede, Colorado. I was reading a free newspaper, curled up on a large couch in a small house on Main Street. That house, which belongs to my parents, sits practically next door to the site of Alice's former workplace—a saloon where she practiced her trade as a professional gambler in 1891, until the place burned down in 1892, along with most of Creede.

The article fascinated me, as did the picture of Poker Alice. Why did the photo of a pickle-faced, white-haired, cigar-chomping old lady grab my heart and spark my imagination? Why did a short article launch me on a journey to learn much more?

Perhaps it was the spirit of Alice herself, wanting somebody to care enough to investigate and tell the truth about her life. Maybe she was tired of legends spun from unfounded rumors or online exaggerations. It was time someone discovered the real Poker Alice.

Alice was an authentic daughter of the Wild West. No wonder so much was written about her that the stories grew into myth. She garnered great press coverage, starting in 1927, and that attention refused to fade after her death in 1930. (The press wasn't quite so supportive in reporting on a certain manslaughter incident in 1913, but that's a story for later pages.)

The first thing I did after gathering a few nuggets of history about Poker Alice Tubbs, was to fictionalize her story, just as many other writers had done before me. She lived in Creede during its boom days, which seemed like the perfect setting for a murder mystery. For years I'd acted with Red Herring Productions, spreading fake murder and mayhem throughout Colorado and other western states. Inspired, I wrote a script set in Creede, mixing real-life figures—Poker Alice, Soapy Smith, and Bat Masterson—with made-up characters based on historical accounts of life in the boomtown.

Alice was one of the script's red herrings, a character with a motive for murder, who existed in the story to throw the audience off track. It's ironic that my eventual quest to find the truth about the Poker Alice was filled with red herrings, false clues that often led nowhere. And the temptation to fictionalize her life was not mine alone. From books to short stories, TV shows to movies—even "journalistic" accounts—most of what's been written about Poker Alice since her death has favored fiction over fact.

I believed everything I read in books, articles, and online before I started to research Alice in earnest, preparing to perform as a historical re-enactor for the Buffalo Bill Birthday celebration in Golden, Colorado. Her story was compelling and made for a lively presentation. Except it was filled with gaps and contradictions.

Was Alice born to the Ivers family in England in 1851 or in 1853? Or was she born in Virginia? Some accounts said Alice was a finishing-school graduate and genius at math. She came to Leadville (or was it Lake City) as a young bride and lost her first husband in a mining accident. One thing was clear—she played poker to support herself and traveled the western mining towns: gambling, winning, moving on. But what about reports that, as a devoted Catholic, she never played poker on a Sunday? Did she truly live in Creede for nearly two years, moving to Deadwood, South Dakota, after the big fire in 1892? Or was she in Deadwood as early as 1876?

As her story grew wilder, I researched and wondered where the truth lay. Which of the many reported events really happened?

Did her second husband, Warren, fall in love with her after she shot an angry gambler who tried to knife Warren as he dealt the game of faro?

Did the couple move to a ranch near Sturgis and raise seven children? Was it true that Warren died of tuberculosis in the middle of a raging blizzard? Had Alice really driven his frozen body to Sturgis and used her poker skills to win the money to pay the undertaker?

Did the aging widow open a poker parlor and house of ill-repute, and later marry her handyman to avoid paying his bill?

Her story seemed too good to be true, and in the years after my first performance as Poker Alice, I started sorting fact from fiction, the myth from the mundane. Though many of the juicy tidbits about her life proved untrue, so much of her story is still fascinating. (Yes, there are holes in Alice's story that remain to be filled today, and I'm still digging as fast as I can.)

The many accounts I found in my initial research were filled with colorful quotations from Alice.

"Play your cards and place your bets. I'll take your money without regrets."

"I thought it would take longer to pay back the loan on my place, but I forgot about that convention of Methodist preachers coming to town."

"At my age, I suppose I should be knitting. But I'd rather play poker with 4 or 5 good players than eat."

Only that last statement was actually one of Alice's, but she had a lot of other colorful things to say about her life in the Wild West.

I understand why there's so much misinformation published about her. It's tough researching a woman who wasn't famous in her day—until the last years of her life. Alice lived during a time when census records weren't always accurate and marriage certificates or personal IDs weren't required. She moved frequently from start-up town to boomtown. Her letters weren't saved and no diary exists. No doubt she edited her own story and may have lied about her name and age here and there. Her fame came in her later years, thanks to articles written by newspaper reporters who sometimes cared more about telling a good story than fact-checking it.

Her ghost is nudging me again. I think she's not too happy about all the untruths I once helped spread. So this book holds as much truth about the real Poker Alice Tubbs's story as I could track down in reliable sources. Join me as we hunt for the truth and dig into the fascinating story of a woman who was way ahead of her time. Poker Alice deserves to be a legend because of her real life in real places that were dangerous and desirable. Meet Alice Ivers Duffield Tubbs Huckert. That might even be her real name!

CHAPTER 1

Lively Lake City Days

Where other women applied feminine rules to their gambling,
I preferred the masculine ones, and learned to be
as stony faced as the rest of them.

POKER ALICE TUBBS, *The Saturday Evening Post*

HER CHOICES DIDN'T LOOK GOOD. Frank was gone and Alice
was on her own, a young widow in a young mining town
surrounded by towering mountains. How would she support
herself now?

The tragedy came without warning. On a day like any other,
in an ordinary mine tunnel, Frank's life ended instantly when a
dynamite charge misfired.[1]

We can imagine what that was like for Alice. In shock, wrapped
in grief, Alice had to get through the funeral and make difficult
decisions—such as where to bury her husband and how to notify
family members back East. The young woman quickly set aside her
grief to deal with practical matters. Her most pressing need was
paying for rent and food without Frank's income or help from far
away family members. What could she do?

There were choices for an attractive young widow like Alice.
But they weren't all good choices, and overall the opportunities
for women to earn a decent living were limited.

Still, in the mid-1870s, Lake City was a thriving community
with more to offer than most. Though isolated by high peaks in

southwestern Colorado, the town boomed while Alice was there. The lure of silver brought masses of people bent on making a fast profit.

Alice herself was caught up in the excitement in the early years of her marriage to Frank Duffield, a mining engineer. Picture Lake City through her own words, as she described the town to a reporter fifty years later:

> A teeming place was Lake City in those days. One knows it now chiefly as the resting place of the three victims of the man known as Packer, the Colorado Cannibal, convicted in the early days of having lured gold seekers into the high Rockies that he might there kill and devour them. But when I arrived, there were other things to talk about—the gold streaming from the hills. There were dance halls and gambling places where women attended as well as men. A thousand and one exciting events were ever present to attract one possessing curiosity and imagination, and I absorbed it all like the proverbial sponge.[2]

The notorious episode involving Alfred Packer took place in 1873, shortly before the town was officially platted in 1874. Packer was eventually captured and convicted of murder after the thawing bodies of five prospectors were discovered a mile from Lake City. The five, led by Packer, had set out on a journey through the San Juan Mountains when they were trapped by heavy snowfall. After many weeks Packer turned up alone at the Los Pinos Indian Agency, with a tale of being beaten by his companions and left for dead. Suspicions landed on Packer when the bodies were found, skulls crushed and corpses mangled and missing pieces of flesh.

Arrested and chained to a rock, Packer managed to escape and elude authorities for nine years. He served time in the Canon City prison, was pardoned after an intensive campaign by the *Denver Post,* and died a natural death in Denver in 1906.

By 1875, the *Silver World* newspaper was promoting Lake City's boom and luring adventure seekers to the area. The town was prospering by 1876 and '77, with some 500 buildings and a population

Saloons in Lake City in the late 1800s and early 1900s were rough places, likely to have patrons as rustic as those shown in this typical establishment. While not in Lake City, Tim Looney's place in Montezuma, Colorado, operated at a high altitude and served miners in a remote mountain area. *Photo credit: The Denver Public Library, Western History Collection, X-11105*

of 2,500 including churches and banks, but no schools.[3] Records from 1878 reveal the city boasted two breweries, 20 saloons, and a "Hell's Acre" of dance halls and brothels.[4]

In September 20, 1876, Lake City residents were thrilled by a visit and speeches from Susan B. Anthony. Her appearance at the Lake City courthouse drew such an overflow crowd that the event was moved outdoors. The September 22, 1876, *Silver World* article describing the event demonstrates that women's rights were already a serious concern for the small town:

The assembly, in which there was a respectable sprinkling of the fair sex, showing that they are interested in this question more than the opponents of the movement would have us believe, stood for two hours in the cool, night air and listened with rapt attention to the speaker who held the multitude with wonderful power. The address was an able and logical appeal in favor of extending the right of suffrage to women. The hearty and enthusiastic affirmative vote given, when we consider the fact that our miners have no squeamishness about expressing their opinions, was sufficient to convince those in attendance that the friends of equal suffrage are by no means so hopelessly in the minority in Hinsdale county as the opponents would have us believe.

With no children to care for, and Frank hard at work in the mines, Alice had plenty of free time. She could have passed her days reading for entertainment. She was well educated, the daughter of a schoolmaster from Sudbury, England (she said). After her parents came to America, they raised their children in the East, far from mining camps and games of chance. But young Alice had a zest for adventure, which made it easier to marry Frank and leave her Eastern home for the unknown west.[5]

As the months in Lake City went by, Alice turned her skill at cards to gambling and won money. She and Frank enjoyed the extra earnings—and he didn't need to worry about his wife's safety in the busy mining town. Alice could take care of herself. She carried a gun in those days—a .38 on a .45 frame—and she knew how to shoot it. She said, "My father had been an excellent marksman and he had passed his knowledge to me. . . . I was not afraid. I went everywhere, the faro and stud games of the gambling halls being my chief lure."[6]

Betting on Herself

After Frank's sudden death, Alice was forced to make a crucial choice. She had to make a living. Her education qualified her to teach school, but Lake City was not exactly an ideal place to raise a family, so it had no schools. Other work in the area involved heavy labor or the more traditional mining town occupations of "soiled doves" and saloon girls. None of those choices appealed to Alice. So she turned to the skill she'd perfected in her free time: playing poker for money. She was young, she was attractive, and she quickly learned how to make her way in a man's world.

Though losing her young husband was a tragedy, the loss marked the beginning of Alice's adventures as a professional gambler. She was in the right place at the right time to live the life she sought. The Colorado Rocky Mountains and surrounding states saw an explosion of boomtowns throughout the 1870s, '80s, and '90s, and Alice was smack dab in the middle of it all—experiencing her personal times of boom and bust, joy and danger, excitement, and challenge.

Losing Frank was a tough experience for the young woman, but little did she know she was about to embark on a life filled with thrill-seeking and risk-taking. Compared to other women of her time, who mostly opted for the safety of marriage or a father's protection in spinsterhood, Alice was a working woman who stayed on the right side of the law. She was not constrained by Victorian customs or oppressed by the standard role assigned to women in her day. A lady of the 1870s through the turn of the century would have been bound by cultural norms, guidelines, and expectations such as these:

> There is beauty in the helplessness of woman. Her first effort at comparative freedom is bitter enough; for the delicate mind shrinks from every unaccustomed contact and the warm and gushing heart closes itself, like the blossom of the sensitive plant, at every approach.
>
> It is a defect of our civilization that women are forced to become breadwinners. Young girls who ought to be training in the school at home for the high and holy duties of wifehood and motherhood are compelled by social and industrial maladjustments to enter the hurly-burly of the

great work-a-day world, competing with those who ought
to support them in the desperate struggle for existence.

The average woman has as much brains as the average
man . . . but the woman lacks endurance in things mental;
her fortitudes are physical and spiritual. She lacks nervous
stability.[7]

Prejudice against women like Alice would have extended
beyond her femininity. Gamblers were distrusted and distained by
members of proper society. *The Guardian* newspaper offered this
warning in 1867: "Young man, beware of gambling and gamblers.
They lead to evil. . . . Shun the whole brood of chance amuse-
ments. They are Satan's trap to catch souls."[8] And ladies who
smoked, as Alice did, were cautioned to keep that filthy habit
private from any public display.

Fortunately for Alice, many people in Lake City and throughout the West looked more favorably on a woman's independence
and equality with men. For example, the *Silver World* newspaper
editorials offered support for women's voting rights in 1877.
Colorado citizens failed to pass the 1877 referendum on women's
right to vote, but women's suffrage was passed in 1893, a quarter of
a century earlier than the national achievement of women's voting
rights in 1920. A strong-minded woman like Alice had a better
opportunity to be herself in the more liberal atmosphere west of
the Mississippi.

Fifty years later, Alice reflected on her past and her reasons
for making unorthodox choices about how she'd live her life. She
knew the path she followed made her a rare woman, and she was
certain about her personal motivations:

"It was the thrill of it, to buck the game and beat the game. . . .
The thrill, in case one may think that I am looking upon memories
from afar, never leaves one."[9]

Alice wasn't famous enough in her day to show up in local newspapers, enabling us to track her movements from town to town. So the next chapter covers more than a decade of her life, without specific years to pin the events on. She was living her story, but the details of her private life would be kept to herself for many decades to come.

No, we can't find many sources to verify when she was in certain towns at certain times. But she said she was there—naming Leadville, Georgetown, Central City, Alamosa, Del Norte, El Paso, Silver City and more—and we can trust her word. She wasn't the type to draw from the bottom of the deck.

Poker Alice traveled to remote areas on trains such as this one crossing a Colorado Midland Railroad bridge above Buena Vista, Colorado. *Lake County Public Library, Colorado Mountain History Collection (Resource ID 1951)*

CHAPTER 2

Betting on the Boomtowns

*I did not stay long at my first job, and never stayed long at any,
in fact; there were too many other games to buck, too many
chances for a big winning, too many camps waiting
to be invaded. The life of a gambler was a life of travel,
the constant excitement of something new.*

POKER ALICE TUBBS, *The Saturday Evening Post*

FROM BOOMTOWN HISTORIES, we can speculate that Alice
Duffield traveled to Leadville in the early 1880s after Lake City's
luster started to dim. While there is no way to know for certain,
routes from Lake City to Leadville were well established, accessible
by rail or stagecoach, and she could have landed in Leadville after
spending time in Buena Vista, Colorado. Initially the new railroad
reached only as far as Buena Vista, and those headed to the silver
camp of Leadville had to catch a stagecoach from there.

We can envision the typical mining boomtowns Alice encountered based on this vivid description written by a traveler in 1880:

> Buena Vista is a new town situated near the headwaters of
> the Arkansas river. This town five months ago had only
> three buildings, it now contains from three to four hundred
> cheap wooden structures, some well built hotels, saloons
> and gambling houses without number. It claims a popula-
> tion of 1500. The town is in the midst of a park country,
> surrounded on all sides by magnificent snow covered

mountains. …Tents greet the eye along the streets in every direction. Large canvas covered buildings, tents filled with merchandise, and mammoth tents transformed into warehouses crammed full of freight supplies en route to Leadville and the Gunnison country are everywhere seen.

Buena Vista has been a lively town for the past four months, being the terminus of the Denver and Rio Grande Railway, the nearest station to Leadville. But the line will have completed a road up the Arkansas from Canon City past this place to Leadville by July 1st, when this place will have to decline.[1]

Known as one of the most lawless towns in the West, the story is told of one house of ill repute along a Buena Vista street with dozens of saloons. Its false front bore a hand-written sign that read "The Mule Skinner's Retreat." Faced with a town full of drifters and others keeping a low profile, the postmistress was hard put to deliver mail sent to questionable characters with unclear addresses. The agreed-upon solution? All mail going to a certain element was dropped into a special box beneath a back window with a missing pane at the Mule Skinner's. Apparently even those "on the lam" were trusted to reach through the window and take their own letters, leaving the rest behind.

A visit to both Lake City and Buena Vista today reveals two towns that appear very similar, nestled on patches of flat land beneath scenic mountains. Alice likely felt right at home in Buena Vista, and she would have had plenty of saloons and gambling halls to choose from. But as a gambler, how could she resist the attraction of nearby Leadville once that storied silver town was up and booming?

Lively Times in Leadville

The best way for Alice to reach the heart of the next boomtown was by rail. A journey in a cramped and dusty stagecoach was a distant second choice. She must have had a good instinct for being

In the mid-1880s, it is very likely Alice played poker at the Texas House, a renowned "gambling resort" on Harrison Avenue in Leadville. *Lake County Public Library, Colorado Mountain History Collection (Resource ID 180)*

in the right place at the right time then moving on when the next crop of poker-playing miners was ready to harvest. When word spread about her honest reputation, it would quickly draw opponents looking to win fair and square against a lady gambler.

Alice played an honest game. She believed cheating took all the fun out of gambling. She told one reporter:

> It was not an outlaw practice to live by one's wits and one's ability to outguess the other person in a contest of cards. Dishonesty and crookedness were not the constant companions of games of chance. The gambler played because he loved it for the thrill of the turn of a card or a tight pinch in a contest with persons as sharp as he. Dishonesty hurt the thrill; when crookedness came to gambling, the real professionals quit, leaving the name to be taken by men—and women—who should have been called professional crooks instead.[2]

Alice was proud to be a professional gambler, and Leadville, Colorado, would have been an ideal town to learn and grow her trade. By 1879 the town had four banks, five churches, about twenty hotels—and eighty-two saloons. By 1880 the town's population was almost 15,000, and it was filled with gambling houses, dance halls and saloons to entertain the mostly-male population.[3]

One thing the busy town lacked was a first-class opera house—a need soon met by wealthy Horace W. Tabor. He donated the land and the money for the Tabor Opera House, which opened on November 20, 1879.[4] If Alice lived in Leadville in the early 1880s, she no doubt would have attended high-altitude performances in the lavishly decorated building.

Musicians, dancers, and Shakespearean actors all made their way to Leadville. Even Irish poet and playwright Oscar Wilde performed there and later said it was the highlight of his American tour. The 2005 book, *High Drama,* describes Wilde's Leadville performance this way:

In 1880, Leadville was growing into a boomtown that would one day rival Denver in population. The 100 block of West Chestnut, shown here, would have been familiar to Alice. *Lake County Public Library, Colorado Mountain History Collection (Resource ID 182)*

He arrived in October 1882 dressed like a miner and immediately was faint from the altitude. Pronounced fit, he appeared that evening on the stage in a cutaway jacket, velvet knee breeches, ruffled shirt and very long hair. ... In the midst of silver miners, he expounded upon Benvenuto Cellini, the sixteenth-century Italian silversmith. Asked why he had not brought Mr. Cellini along, Wilde explained that he was long dead, to which an audience member queried, "Who shot him?"[5]

By 1883, Leadville began to decline as silver production leveled off. Ten years later, the town's fortunes fell sharply after the Panic of 1893 caused a serious depression across the United States and lowered the price of silver.

Despite the downturn, Alice had no problem finding work elsewhere. She knew she could find a job at any of a dozen big gambling halls in the West. Why? Not only was she good, she was special, a novelty. She explained:

> A feminine handler of cards meant an attraction to any house, and a salary of twenty-five dollars a night awaited me practically wherever I cared to work. This was a high wage, with a good reason behind its payment. Of women gamblers there were indeed few, simply because the average woman, though she is a gambler at heart, hasn't the face for wagering anything but affections. She has too many nerves, too many temptations to display her joy when she has a good hand or her sorrow at a bad one. The true gambler remains the same under all circumstances. I've won just as many big pots on a pair of deuces and a good bluff as I have on a royal flush. But the usual feminine instinct prohibits the poker face, and without a countenance that can remain immobile for hour after hour, professional gambling is useless—except to an opponent.[6]

Mining towns close to Denver were easily reached by train, and Alice traveled by rail to fill her hand with cards and winnings. Central City was second only to Denver in population in 1870, surpassed by Leadville ten years later in 1880.[7] Central City had its own renowned opera house, considered by many to be the most beautiful in the state of Colorado.

When Alice arrived at some point in the 1880s, Central City wasn't all that new, having been platted in 1860. The thriving town laid claim to "the richest square mile on earth." The main downtown was almost destroyed by fire in 1874, but that just gave rise to new building and eventually more permanent structures, some of which stand today.[8] The Central City Opera House continues to host performances, and a visit today offers the same view Alice enjoyed when she attended in her day.

High Stakes in the Rockies

Established mountain towns such as Central City would have offered better lodging and gambling venues for Alice, but she had no qualms about more rustic offerings. She described the standard gambling hall as a humble place. Typically she would be paid to work for the house as a dealer, though she often returned during her "off hours" to gamble and win for herself.

Looking back, she painted a detailed picture of her typical workplace:

> When the term "gambling hall" is mentioned, it all too often brings the picture of a garish place, beautifully furnished—perhaps according to the ideas of Monte Carlo or the establishments which once existed in New York. The frontier gambling hall was of a far different order. In the first place, the need for haste was too great for any time to be wasted upon furnishings. Then, too, the gambling hall of the frontier mining camp almost invariably grew before the rail road, with the result that it often was of logs, with a sawed floor for dancing, a bar at one side and the games placed where there could be the best light and the most opportunity to play.[9]

In mining towns, dealers often worked in shifts—from noon until six, six until twelve, and then the graveyard shift from twelve at night until six o'clock in the morning. Alice preferred to work from noon until six in the evening so she could use the rest of the night to play in card games with somebody else dealing.

Not far from Central City lies a town that was once considered the most important silver camp in Colorado. Georgetown was born of the gold rush in 1859, but it truly boomed in size and energy during the silver mining days of the late 1870s and early '80s. At some point Alice's travels brought her there, and she might even have wished to stay at the elegant Hotel de Paris.

The hotel was founded by Louis Du Puy, a native of France, who was quite an eccentric. In 1875 he remodeled the Delmonico

Alice gambled with willing miners and with the merchants who sold them supplies and entertainment in busy Georgetown. *Supply Train for the Argentine, (2000.129.139), History Colorado*

Bakery on Alpine Street into the lavishly furnished Hotel de Paris, still standing today. While it's not established that DuPuy refused all women the right to spend the night there, he accepted only those guests who passed his close scrutiny. Some he turned away for no apparent reason.[10]

Did Alice gain entry? With her education and ladylike demeanor, she would have had a gambler's chance at least.

Just upriver, the town nearest Georgetown was Silver Plume—also a silver mining camp in Clear Creek County. It would have been simple for Alice to play poker against eager and often lonely miners while she lived in Georgetown. The life of a miner was not easy. One story is often told of a solitary miner in Silver Plume, an Englishman named Griffin. He discovered the Seven-Thirty Mine and grew rich from its heavy deposits of silver and gold. Yet he didn't squander his money in town; instead he spent his spare time playing his violin or carving out a grave-shaped depression facing his cabin on Columbia Mountain.

> Each evening, after his stint of excavating the refractory rock, Griffin would bring out his violin to play the melodies and classical music of earlier days. One June night in '87 the miners thought he played particularly well. Then they heard a shot reverberating in the canyon. Face down in the grave with a bullet in his heart, was the gentleman from Picadilly.[11]

From central Colorado, Alice could have easily traveled by train to the southern part of the state, and taken up residence, at least temporarily, in Trinidad, Alamosa, and Del Norte—all prosperous and thriving towns that offered the thrill of the game and a constant influx of new players.

Trinidad's attraction for Alice in her roaming days was that it was a lively railroad town and filled with workers who labored in the area's rich coal mines. In the 1880s famous tough guy Bat Masterson was a town marshal. His favorite pastime of gambling might have caused him to cross paths with Alice there, if not later when both were in Creede. Wyatt Earp drove the stage between Trinidad and Box Springs, New Mexico, and Kit Carson was frequently in the area. Another independent woman lived in Trinidad around the same time as Alice. Cathay Williams was the only woman known to have served with the Buffalo Soldiers after changing her name to William Cathay and dressing like a man, lived in Trinidad after her discharge.[12]

The town of Alamosa, located in the San Luis Valley, is today known for tourism, education, and its many surrounding farms and ranches. In Alice's day it was also a busy railroad hub that started with the arrival of the railroad on July 4, 1878. By 1890 and for fifty years, Alamosa was the center of narrow gauge railroading in America. In the 1880s, a "ditch boom" contributed to the Alamosa's economic success. Eastern investors were interested in putting their money into irrigation canals and Travelers Insurance

Company of Connecticut built a number of large canals, allowing Alamosa and the San Luis Valley area to grow exponentially. Men, and women like Alice, looking to make quick money, were drawn to Alamosa and nearby towns by the growth.[13]

The San Juan Mountains were found to be rich in gold and silver deposits starting in the mid-1870s. Situated at the west end of the San Luis Valley, the town of Del Norte became a major supply base and financial center, and it was the county seat for Rio Grande County. As its boom years of the 1880s swelled the population to some 10,000 residents, the town featured an opera house, library, dance halls, and of course, the saloons where Alice would have made her stake. The thriving town was her base in early 1891 before she left on a hazardous journey—racing to be one of the first to settle at the foot of massive cliffs rich with promise.[14]

Playing Her Cards Right

Recalling her decades of successful gambling, and the excitement it brought to her life, in her old age Alice recognized that those were her gambling glory days—days long gone.

As she got older, honest players were harder to come by, and Alice complained to a reporter that the game had changed because of cheating. "It is still good to play, still a thrill to look at the faces about a table and to know that you are matching your brains against those of men with whom card playing is a passion. But I want those men, in these new and hectic days, to be ones with years of friendship behind them. Otherwise I obey the signs in the Pullman cars: Don't play cards with strangers."[15]

Many strangers were still destined to play against Alice as the decade of the 1880s drew to a close. As she practiced her poker face and grew in confidence, she depended on a steady flow of new acquaintances to pay her bills as she turned eastward and headed for the flatlands.

CHAPTER 3

Gambling in the Flatlands

*I had set my poker face and chewed my big black cigar
and brought the cards from the faro box in practically every
big camp of the West before this time. I simply cite the journey
as an instance of what the gambler of the old days—man or
woman—would undergo to reach a new camp and to be
on the ground floor when the boom really broke.*

POKER ALICE TUBBS, *The Saturday Evening Post*

F ROM HER EARLY TWENTIES well into her thirties, Alice was a nomad, spending a year or two in each boomtown before moving on. Did she travel alone? Was she lonely for the company of a man? Did she wish to marry again? Or was the thrill of adventure romance enough as the years and new vistas added up?

Marriage would be in the cards for Alice again—not just once, but twice. But when? Piecing together the picture of Alice's love life is complicated by a confusing paper trail. Based on her own accounts, it's very likely she didn't marry again until her early forties. If she had more casual relationships, she never spoke of them publicly. Her days in Kansas and Oklahoma appear to have been spent as independently as her years in the mountain towns. No matter where she roamed, she lived in a state of freedom she clearly found comfortable.

Her good looks continued to be a draw and she dressed in fashionable gowns and glittering jewelry to send a message that she was a serious professional, and a successful one.

Taken some time between 1870 and 1890, this photograph shows a Chicago, Rock Island and Pacific Railroad locomotive and coal car in front of the depot in Caldwell, Kansas. Poker Alice would have alighted more than once from a train at this depot. *Denver Public Library, Western History Collection, X-22227*

Off to the Flatlands

In 1889, Caldwell, Kansas, was known as a reckless and wild cow town, nicknamed "the Border Queen" for its proximity to the Oklahoma state line. It soon gained a new reputation as a key jumping off place for the Land Run of 1889.[1] That year, starting April 22, an estimated 50,000 people rushed to claim land for 9,000 homesteads in Oklahoma.[2]

In the spring of 1889, as ambitious settlers camped in Kansas state-line towns like Caldwell, ambitious gamblers like Alice joined them for reasons of their own. Her goal wasn't land; it was landing fat purses. As she put it:

> I suppose I might be a member of the pioneers' society of Oklahoma if it were not for one thing. When that country opened in '89, I made the rush in there, driving alone in

a buggy from Caldwell, Kansas, across the Cherokee Strip and down through the rugged territory into what is now Oklahoma. But I didn't go there to build a farm from the wilderness. There would be new towns, thousands of men with money in their pockets and but few diversions. Some of these men would be shrewd at cards and some of them would only think they were shrewd. A good harvest during the opening days of Oklahoma did not come for two years —except for persons like myself. Our harvest came at once; we had gone there to gamble.[3]

By the time she drove a wagon to Oklahoma, Alice was truly a capable woman in a man's world. No matter her location, she attracted crowds of ready opponents who were convinced a woman would be easy to beat. Though she took their money, she offered novelty in return. Sometimes lonely miners and cowboys were merely glad for a chance to sit and stare at a pretty, if motionless, face. Alice dressed in the top fashions of the day and remained feminine in the roughest conditions known mostly to men. Though she was a rarity, she wasn't alone among lady gamblers in frontier outposts.

Lively Lady Gamblers

Alice's path crossed those of other Western women gamblers. A half dozen are remembered by their colorful names: Poker Nell, Madame Mustache, Airship Annie, China Mary, Haltershanks Eva, and Bowlegged Mary.[4]

She felt sorry for one gambling friend, a woman she described as home-loving and quiet, who was stuck with an unflattering nickname. This sweet woman—apparently blessed with a robust figure—was christened the Iowa Bull. Fortunately, Alice avoided an uncomplimentary nickname, though she had a brush with one of the dullest nicknames ever—Corduroy Alice. Eventually "Poker Alice" stuck and she escaped being forever remembered for a sturdy fabric or an unusual physical feature.

Eleanor Dumont, the famous lady gambler known
as Madame Moustache, and Poker Alice were friends.
LegendsofAmerica.com

Of all the female gamblers she met, Madame Mustache was the
one Alice found most interesting. Why Madame Mustache? Alice
explained it to reporter Courtney Ryley Cooper: "They called her
that for the simple reason that she possessed a mustache—at least,
a line of coal-black hair upon her upper lip, enhanced of course
by her femininity . . . Madame Mustache was Madame because
she was French."

Alice considered Madame Mustache a remarkable woman.
She said of her, "We knew no more of her than that she had come
from France with her husband and almost immediately taken up
the profession of gambling, with a leaning toward faro. She was a
musician and a linguist, with the ability to speak five languages.
I have often found myself wondering what her beginnings might
have been and what had led her into the gambling halls. But then

I have heard the same things about myself. The love of cards, the thrill of the play—these are reasons enough."

Adventure was the common ground these ladies shared. "There were many such adventurous women as Madame Mustache and myself who were in the West on their own, many a girl who now, in her old age, may be a feminine pillar of a church or the head of a local literary society, with her past fully buried."[5]

Stories too Good to Check?

Did Alice really travel to all the places she claimed and have the adventures she described in her later years? Some writers dismissed her as a minor player in the story of women gamblers of the Wild West. In fact, in his 1927 book, *Calamity Jane and the Lady Wildcats,* writer Duncan Aikman wrote Alice off in a single paragraph:

> On the outskirts of Deadwood Poker Alice still lives. But in spite of her many merits Poker Alice appears to belong to the type on which spurious legends of gambling Amazons are founded. Often in the bold, wide open days, she strolled into some gaudy sportsman's paradise and broke the bank in sheer delight of pasteboard battle. Often in her own houses of entertainment after the serious pleasure of the evening was over she has refreshed favored friends with games which have put a considerable strain on their credit if not on the friendship. But although her zest, skill and fortunes are properly famous, Poker Alice has functioned only as a patron of professionals and—a tactful hostess.[6]

No doubt Aikman knew of Alice as the hostess of her own establishment. But his words are a blunt dismissal of the role Alice played among her peers throughout the West. Aikman's book was written and published before Alice gained national fame through a sensational *Saturday Evening Post* profile and subsequent newspaper articles.

Based on the details Alice shared about the people and the world she knew for decades, we can confidently conclude that she

was an insider. For Aikman to dismiss her as a mere "patron" and
"tactful hostess" indicates that he either neglected to do his home-
work, or found Alice less interesting than the legendary Calamity
Jane (about whom much fiction was presented as fact during and
after her heyday). If he had interviewed Alice in depth, or at all,
he may have been inclined to change his mind.

The Games Alice Played to Win

Throughout the years, certain card games were familiar to Alice
and others in the gambling halls. Not all forms of poker known
today had been created, and the most common in the West was
Five-card Draw.

Historians date the birth of poker to the early 1800s, and it was
widely played by 1829. While the earliest form was played with 20
cards and no draw, it was soon challenged by the 52-card version
in the mid 1830s. The first mention of Draw Poker, the game Alice
mastered, occurs in the 1850 edition of Bohn's New Handbook
of Games. By 1875, Draw, Stud, and Jack Pots all appear in The
American Hoyle. Texas Hold'em wouldn't come along for decades.[7]

Faro was another popular gambling game in Alice's day.
Playing the game was sometimes known as "bucking the tiger."
(*Buck* was slang for a win.) Quoted in *The Saturday Evening Post,*
Alice provided a short history lesson on the origins of the game:
"In spite of the general belief that faro is a strictly American game
… it is not American. It is of French beginnings and the name
came from "Pharaoh," because on the backs of the French cards
with which it originally was played was the picture of an Egyptian
king."

With its fast action, easy-to-learn-rules, and better odds than
most games of chance, faro was popular in every gambling hall in
the West. Played with a single deck of cards and allowing for any
number of players, faro requires a dealer, called a banker, and a
board that displays one card of each denomination. The dealer lays
out cards from a special box and as the game commences, each
player lays his stake on one or more cards.

The faro dealer, usually employed by the house, places the "banker's card" on the right, and the "player's card" on the left. The banker wins all the money staked on the banker's card, while paying double the sums staked to those betting on the player's card. For many years, faro provided no significant edge to the house, but later widespread cheating by rigging the dealer's box put an end to faro's popularity.[8]

The Importance of Staying Lucky

Alice played fair and won because she played with skill when it counted and was lucky when she needed to be. Like many other gamblers, she had her own superstitions about staying on the side of Lady Luck. One superstition she held was that good luck depended on being generous with her winnings. She told a reporter:

> If I had today the money that I have passed out during my lifetime as I turned from lucky sessions at poker or faro, I would be rich. But I'm just as glad I haven't it; there would have been in its place the memory of empty hands and gaunt faces to haunt me.
>
> They were always present, those outstretched hands, those expectant countenances, when a lucky player turned to leave—the hands and features of those who had bucked the tiger and found that animal invincible. We had a rule in those days—perhaps a dollar, perhaps five; we would dole it out like a persona dispensing tips in a foreign hotel. Superstition played its part, too; we might not be lucky next time if we forgot an unfortunate.[9]

When the excitement of the plains cities died down, Alice knew it was time to move on. Timing was a big part of her success. No doubt she read the newspapers avidly, always on the lookout for a new town ripe for picking. Sometimes she was anxious to get in on the ground floor. Other journeys brought her to towns settled enough "for a woman with quick eyes and a poker face to make a living." As Alice said, "Flush times are the harvest times for a professional gambler." [10]

Turning back to Colorado in 1890, Alice quickly became among the first gamblers to hit pay dirt in that little, but legendary, town called Creede.

CHAPTER 4

Adventures in Creede
and Bachelor

Gamblers all, we were in those days. Some played their games
with pawns of merchandise or cattle or with the pick and pan
in search of gold. I preferred my game to be that of cards.

POKER ALICE TUBBS, *The Saturday Evening Post*

IN JANUARY OF 1891, Alice joined a handful of prospectors on
a risky journey through the San Juan Mountains. She left Del
Norte, Colorado, in the dead of winter just to be in on the ground
floor of a brand new boomtown. At first the place was called King
Solomon's Mines. As it grew along a massive box canyon at the
junction of North and South Willow Creek, the town formerly
known as Willow was soon called Jim Town and—where it clung
to the creek bed—String Town. Ultimately, all joined under the
name Creede, a tribute to Nicolas Creede, the man who first struck
it rich there.[1]

Alice was still in her thirties, and hardy enough to brave the
hazards of this daring adventure. Here's how she described it to
reporter Courtney Ryley Cooper:

There was no trail; there was no shelter save overhanging
cliffs, reflecting the blazing heat of a tremendous log fire at
night; there was only the food that was carried on one's
back and the small game that dropped to one's rifle.

Not long after Poker Alice arrived in Creede, structures such as the Cliff Hotel were hastily constructed. In 1881, this two-story hotel was located near the junction of East and West Willow Creeks. The rock formation behind the hotel remains a prominent landmark today. *Photo courtesy of the Creede Historical Society*

But, after all, these difficulties mattered little. Gold— and silver—was in the offing; money to be gained from the ground by three miners, and for the fourth member of the party, a woman, the hope of a big stake in the turn of a card or the threat of a stack of chips, shoved to the center of the table at the climactic moment of a game of draw poker.[2]

What might that journey have been like for a woman closer to 40 than 30? Getting in on the ground floor of a brand new boomtown must have been a powerful motivator for the trip. What did she bring with her? How did she transport her professional wardrobe? Perhaps pack mules were used to carry supplies and help travelers get established in an unsettled area. They arrived in winter at the mouth of a box canyon fronted by massive cliffs; at least the location offered a steady source of creek water and some protection from the wind.

For Alice, no town before or after compared to Creede. It was an untamed place of unlimited opportunity. Why was Creede so special? She gave one reporter her reasons:

> An atmosphere was present in that town which to my mind has never been equaled save by the excitement of the Oklahoma rush, in which cities grew overnight and a place like Oklahoma City, only a station on the Santa Fe Railroad in the morning was by midnight of the same day a complete little city, with portable houses set up on lots which had been claimed by the boomers, with a government under way, and stores, speak-easies and gambling halls running as though they had been in operation for weeks.
>
> Creede was like that—a town which came into being so swiftly that the transition seemed next to impossible. ... Night and day, day and night, it grew, and by night and day it blared and blustered and celebrated. Keys were never turned in the locks; there were few locks for a key to enter. Gambling tables were set up in the streets; the crowds in the halls were so great as to impede play there.[3]

That Crazy Place Called Creede

By the end of 1891, people were rushing to Creede. Several trains a day pulled into the station, with men clinging to the sides of the cars. Others drove teams or came on horseback or burro, and many walked there, using the railroad beds as trails. All were looking for a chance to make their fortunes. The town was so crowded that the Pullman Company sidetracked sleeping cars and charged men a dollar a night to sleep on the floor with blankets. Almost instantly, businesses, hotels, and restaurants sprang up and were open well into the night. Saloons and gambling houses did not close at all.[4]

North Creede was the original town site of Creede Camp. The town spilled into the lower canyon, and that area was called Stringtown. Just like Alice in the early 1890s, the town followed the railroad. *Photo courtesy of the Creede Historical Society*

Creede's legendary growth quickly brought a wealth of gamblers to Alice's table. As a firsthand observer, she knew that "a mining camp in its flush days is hysteria personified." She told her *Saturday Evening Post* interviewer, "Something for nothing—that seems to be the general belief; and because of that hallucination, men will endure hardships, bad living conditions and discomforts in perfect happiness, chancing life's savings without a thought, when, under other conditions, they would devote weeks of study before investing a tenth of the sum. Creede was the epitome of such camps."

In her later years, Alice recalled that it was not unusual to see two strangers meet, converse for perhaps a half hour, and then, without putting anything in writing, complete a business deal involving thousands of dollars.

She also gambled in Bachelor, a town populated by miners, located a thousand feet above Creede and equal in size. She said,

Located high above Creede and the mines, the booming town of Bachelor had many gambling establishments. Alice would have gotten her exercise walking between the two towns. The Bachelor residents in the photograph lived apart from the saloons and gambling halls. They appear to have dressed up for this photo opportunity. *Courtesy of the Creede Historical Society*

"There grew into being, high on the mountains above Creede, a rival city called Bachelor, where hammers clanged by night and day and life ran ceaselessly at a most turbulent pitch. Gambling halls were there, too, and a paying mine. I dealt faro and played poker in Bachelor when the predictions were common that this town would outrival Creede and for that matter form the great metropolis of Southern Colorado. There would be smelters and a railroad running over the top of the mountains, great buildings, and wide streets."[5]

Alice worked a mid-day shift for various saloon owners, usually from noon to six at night. Even during these daylight hours, she encountered danger. One evening, returning to her little log cabin in the semi-darkness, shots whizzed around her. She could barely see two men, each hiding behind woodpiles, firing revolvers at each other.

She ran to the nearest saloon, an easy choice for refuge since they were everywhere in town. Pounding on Steve Scribner's door, she pushed it to get in. At the same time, Scribner was pushing the door closed to lock it as the shooting accelerated.

"Let me in," she shouted. "It's only Poker Alice!"

Scribner let her in and slammed shut the door as the shooting grew more intense. Suddenly, the noise of gunfire ended as the sound of wailing began.

"I'm a son of a gun!" said Scribner in the darkness. "Is that one of those fellows who's just been shooting to kill? He's bawling like a baby!"

Next, Alice and Scribner heard these words: "Don't shoot any more! Don't shoot any more! You've knocked both of my thumbs off!"

The life-and-death struggle ended. "Listen to the big baby cry!" shouted the man's opponent.

Alice opened the door—only to hear spectators taunting the injured man as they emerged from barricades and spots of safety. She later said, "The howling man, mourning the loss of his thumbs, found himself the owner of a new nickname. He was Baby Joe and Baby Joe he stayed as long as I can remember."[6]

That wasn't the only violence Alice witnessed in Creede or in other mining camps. Yet these events seem to have had little effect on her, caught up as she was in a rough and tumble world. In frontier towns like Creede, human life was held more lightly. Why? Alice's answer was, "The ties of civilization had been cut. Existence was running largely upon a new order and a different deal. It was the fashion to wear one's life upon one's sleeve."[7]

One day in Creede Alice received an invitation to a funeral. It was just that—an invitation that hinted of a grand time to be had by all. The host of the party was the dearly departed. It was a certain gambler's last wish that he should depart this world in the same way that he had lived—a short but happy season.

In the afternoon the entire gambling community, the departed gambler in his coffin leading the crowd, paraded to the cemetery

high on a hill. The town boss and chief criminal operator, Soapy
Smith, acted as toastmaster. Food and refreshments were shared,
along with jokes and laughter, before champagne corks popped.
The crowd drank a toast to their late friend. After his coffin was
placed in the ground, the group returned to Creede and resumed
their lives of chance in a town that knew no night.[8]

Notorious Companions

Alice worked and played in Creede for a year and a half, and
formed some interesting friendships during that time. One man
she admired was the infamous Jefferson "Soapy" Smith. Though
Smith had been drummed out of Denver for his criminal activities,
Alice viewed him through a softer lens when she knew him in
Creede. In her eyes Smith was a "humorous, kindly, generous
fellow who never refused a plea for help and was every ready to
aid an unfortunate."[9]

In addition to her personal dealings with Soapy Smith, Alice
may have been convinced of his kind nature by something that
happened to a visiting parson who ran into trouble. Pastor Tom
Uzzell preached in Creede in April 1892. He collected $75 after
delivering a rousing sermon from the top of a pool table. That
night, thieves broke into his hotel room and stole his money and
his pants. When Smith heard the story the next day, he had his
"boys" run down the guilty parties and force them to give back
the money, the pants, plus a little extra for Uzzell's trouble.[10]

It was a well-publicized helping hand. Unfortunately, rather
than regularly helping the needy, the con man was more often
ready to help the local citizens part with their hard-earned cash.

Alice must have been amused by the gamble Soapy took to get
his hands on a certain Colonel Stone, otherwise known as "The
Petrified Man." Until the eerie figure was nearly revealed as a hoax,
the attraction lured throngs of the curious into Soapy's gambling
hall, ripe for fleecing. No doubt Alice had a peek at the Petrified
Man herself, but she knew better than to play the rigged games
offered by Smith and friends.

A crowd of Creede citizens stand in front of Bob Ford's tent saloon preparing to take his body to the undertaker. The death of Bob Ford was not only a big event in Creede, it made national news. *Photo courtesy of the Creede Historical Society*

The "man" (also called "McGinty" in the *Creede Candle* newspaper), was "discovered" by one Bob Fitzsimmons, a Creede gambler and bunco artist. He claimed he found the petrified body of a man buried in the mud along Farmer's Creek. Fitzsimmons insisted it was a lost member of the Fremont Party from four decades earlier. He hauled McGinty back to town to display at the Vaughn Hotel. Crowds lined up to see the Petrified Man, paying twenty-five cents for a look.

At some point Soapy Smith moved in for a piece of the action and after a ruckus that involved "some lively discussion with fists and guns," the Petrified Man became a fixture in Soapy's place, the Orleans Club. Displayed in the back of the building, under flickering kerosene lamps, the figure's crumbling concrete form wasn't obvious to visitors. When even low lighting couldn't hide the fakery, Soapy leased McGinty to a circus that toured the United States. Finally, after the Smithsonian expressed interest, McGinty disappeared.[11]

Alice was friendly with a man even more famous than Soapy Smith in his day. She spent time with Bob Ford, known throughout the world as the killer of Jesse James. Alice worked as a dealer in Bob Ford's saloon. It didn't take long before she believed he was innocent of the murder accusation—no matter what truth had been widely accepted in the years before they met.

Alice described Ford as "an unobtrusive, commonplace persona of the down-Missouri type, and with none of the heralded mock bravado which he is said to have assumed after the killing of the Missouri bandit leader. More than that, to me at least, he denied that he was the slayer he was charged with being."

Alice often talked to her employer about Jesse James's death. She said, "Ford seemed as anxious to confide in someone as I was anxious to have him talk. His plaint was always that he did not fire the shot which killed Jesse James, and that it was not even his plot thus to remove the bandit leader."

According to Alice, Ford blamed his brother Charlie, who, some time following the murder, committed suicide. Ford told Alice he was always afraid of Jesse and that "if I ever had aimed a gun at him, I would have trembled so I could not have hit him. But Charlie was different, and he is the one who fired the shot. Of course, I was in on the killing—I was there, and I knew that it was going to happen. But Charlie is the one who did the actual shooting—I didn't have the courage." [12]

Was Ford telling Alice the truth? She believed him, but most people didn't. Especially not Ned O'Kelly, who showed up in Ford's gambling hall on June 8, 1892.

Alice was there as an eyewitness to one of Creede's most famous killings. The event took place just three days after a devastating fire, and was possibly the final straw that ended her season in the out-of-control boomtown.

She reported that she had just finished her shift and was standing near the bar where Bob Ford was drinking. She heard Ford's wife call to him, and he turned to answer, walking to the middle of the dance floor as someone else shouted his name from the doorway.

Creede Avenue before the June 1892 fire destroyed all the buildings in this photograph. The hardware business on the right may have been an even better bet than Alice's gambling business considering the original booming of the town was followed by rebuilding after the fire. *Photo courtesy of the Creede Historical Society*

Next, the sound of a shotgun blast rang in her ears. Ford dropped to the floor, his head nearly torn from his neck by the force of the blast fired by Ned O'Kelly. Bob Ford was dead. The town was not sorry to see him go. Alice wisely kept her feelings to herself as others celebrated the death of the widely hated "coward" who killed legendary Jesse James by shooting him in the back.[13]

Away from the Ashes

Ultimately, it was "natural causes" that prompted Alice to pack up her cards and look for a new home. The way she tells it, fire was a natural cause in every mining town like Creede:

> Cabins were erected upon the most accessible places; if four or five of them abutted to form a fire trap, little thought was given the fact. The occupants would have their millions and be gone before the eventuality occurred. So it was in

Creede—wooden sidewalks; wooden, unpainted buildings; trash and rubbish in piles existed throughout the entire bottle shape of the town. The fire started in the neck of the bottle—quite an appropriate place for the Creede of those days—and spread as only a fire could travel in such a thoroughly inflammable place. There was an ironical aspect to it. Creede had reached the place where it saw itself as a metropolis of the future. Fire apparatus had been ordered and that day received, standing red and resplendent upon the depot platform. That burned too![14]

The massive fire on June 5, 1892, damaged many of the town's businesses, and though she could have found another job, a few days after Ford was killed, Alice was ready to go. Still, she would always hold a place in her heart and fond memories of the town that wouldn't stop.

The editor of the *Creede Candle,* Cy Warmen, wrote a poem that soon became nationally famous. It captured the essence of Colorado's renowned boomtown and the men and women like Alice who staked their futures there.

> *The cliffs are solid silver,*
> *With wondrous wealth untold;*
>
> *The beds of its running rivers*
> *Are lined with purest gold.*
>
> *While the world is filled with sorrow,*
> *And hearts must break and bleed*
>
> *It's day all day in the daytime,*
> *And there is no night in Creede.*[15]

This view of lower West Main Street in Deadwood is one Poker Alice would have known well when she gambled there. *South Dakota State Historical Society, South Dakota Digital Archives (2009-01-28-010)*

CHAPTER 5

Starting Over in Deadwood

The lure of the wandering life came back after [Creede]. Other camps
beckoned, among them Deadwood and Lead, in the heart of the last
frontier of America's various mining rushes, the Black Hills.

POKER ALICE TUBBS, *The Saturday Evening Post*

U SING INTERVIEWS AND CENSUS RECORDS to reassemble the
jigsaw puzzle of Alice's life, we can deduce that during this
next season of her life started in 1892 in Deadwood, South Dakota,
where Alice acquired her second husband, Warren G. Tubbs.[1]

A thorough search has failed to turn up a marriage certificate
between Alice Ivers Duffield and Warren G. Tubbs. This document
would solve the mystery about when Alice met Warren, and the
question of whether they were together earlier than 1892—as some
newspaper articles and early biographies have indicated. Yet in
telling her story, Alice was clear that she went to Kansas and
Oklahoma alone, and none of her accounts of her time in Creede
mention a husband. Census records that mention Warren place
him in South Dakota in previous years, so it follows that she met
him there.

Alice must have believed this marriage was in the cards for
her, in spite of Warren's flaws. And, as for the housepainter who
gambled on the side, he'd met his match in Alice. She said:

At last I did the inevitable thing—I remarried, this time a
man who called himself a gambler. Eventually, however,

I wakened to an important fact. My husband had better skill as a house painter, laboring at it in the daytime, and then at night (giving up his) meager earnings before the faro box.

"Look here," I told him one day as we prepared to leave for Silver City, New Mexico, "when any man has to work in the daytime to gamble at night, there's something wrong. You're a good husband, but a rotten gambler. After this, if there's any gambling to be done in this family, I'll do it."[2]

She Broke the Bank

In Silver City, Alice said, "Luck sat on my shoulders." The mining town had been booming for over a decade by the 1890s, and it was easily reached on the Santa Fe Railroad from major towns in the West. The tale of how Poker Alice broke the bank in Silver City turns up frequently in accounts of her life. But the story is best enjoyed through her own words:

> While my husband watched, I placed a small bet and won. Then I won again; soon I was betting the limit of twenty-five dollars, the crowd of onlookers thickening as the play progressed. Several hours passed, with fortune running first to me, then to the house and finally once more in my direction. At last the dealer leaned back in the table.
>
> "The bank's open again," I announced excitedly. "And the limit's off!"
>
> It was a gambler's hunch—to force my luck. I had won a little more than $900 as a player; perhaps I could do as well or better by banking the game. It seemed that the whole gambling hall surged toward me. Though it was the privilege of a player to take the bank once he had broken the dealer, it was unusual, to say the least, for a woman to believe herself capable of handling the rather intricate work of dealing the game, for faro is not a simple affair. There is the deal to handle, as the cards are taken from the box, the

keeping of cases and the watching of the bets upon the layout, usually accomplished by a lookout; but there I was handling everything.

The word spread that a fool woman had taken off the limit and was willing to buck the entire town, and soon enough everyone in the mining camp of Silver City who possessed a gambling instinct had become arrayed against me. It was my first venture as a professional faro dealer and it settled the question of my occupation for many years to come.[3]

When that night's play ended, Alice had won $6000. That money was just begging to be spent, so she and Warren took a sudden and whirlwind trip to New York City.

Alice had visited New York more than once during her years in the gambling business. She said the stages and trains could not run fast enough to get her there. The city fascinated her with its stores, theaters, cafes, and culture. It was the perfect place to spend her winnings before returning to a more rustic lifestyle.

Was Alice ever tempted to stay in the big city? It's doubtful. New York could never give her what she really needed. Her trips there were exciting, but short lived. "Soon I was back in the mining camps with plenty of new clothes, grand memories and an exceedingly lean pocketbook. The latter counted for little. The thrill of gambling was left, and that was all-sufficient."[4]

Dressing for Success

Trips to New York weren't just vacations. They were business trips that enabled Alice to load up on a key tool of her work: an extensive wardrobe.

Alice had appearances to keep up. As a woman, and a player in the upper strata of professional gamblers, she wore the uniform of success. For her, that meant ballroom-style gowns. These high fashion outfits set her apart as a lady as well as an opponent worthy of a gambler's challenge. No doubt the low-cut necklines

The beautiful Fairmont Hotel, at 628 Main Street in Deadwood, featured a gambling parlor where Alice would have enjoyed gaming dressed in her finest. The hotel still stands today in a town that's seen it all. *South Dakota State Historical Society, South Dakota Digital Archives (2008-05-23-022)*

showed off her womanly charms and attracted players who might also enjoy an attractive view.

According to Alice, there were different levels of gamblers, just as there were levels of society and levels available within other professional occupations. She explained to reporter Courtney Ryley Cooper:

> The true gambler would no more associate with the tin-horn, the booster, the hanger-on or the white-chip player than he would draw to a pair of deuces with a royal flush against him. He professed to be a gentleman. As a rule, he was educated; he must possess more than ordinary acumen to follow the profession which he had chosen, he was often courtly, and by his dress was his station known.
>
> In fact, a gambler of the olden type was self-advertised by his clothing the moment he stepped from the stage. His top hat, his carefully modeled boots, unmarred by scratch or scurf and polished to mirror-like brightness, his broad-cloth suit with its Prince Albert coat, his flowing necktie— these were the habiliments of the true upper-crust gambler, and he was not properly dressed unless he wore them.
>
> A few, like Rube Curry and Curly Bill, added a double breasted brocaded vest to their sartorial spectacle, and of course there was always the heavy gold watch chain, often constructed of solid nuggets connected by small links of gold. The rule for the woman gambler, though her number was vastly smaller, demanded as great care and grooming.[5]

In later years, Alice would have to sell off her fancy wardrobe to help make ends meet. In her seventies, she was known for wearing another type of uniform consisting of an ordinary skirt, an olive-drab shirt obtained from the army commissary department, and a military field hat. These served for working in her garden and for hunting and fishing excursions, but at the height of her career, it was silks, satins, and lace for Poker Alice.[6]

Calamity Jane in 1895 at the height of her fame as a Wild West character. *Courtesy Deadwood History, Inc., Adams Museum Collection, Deadwood, SD*

Though the most famous occupants of Deadwood were gone by the 1890s (Wild Bill Hickok had been killed in a gunfight in 1876), some remained. Alice had known Calamity Jane, having met her at Fort Fetterman in the mid-1890s. When she ran into her again in Deadwood, Calamity Jane was well past her prime, but made famous through newspaper accounts of the Wild West and dime novels. By the time Alice encountered her again, Calamity was selling postcards to tourists on the streets.[7]

About Those Big Black Cigars

Most articles about Poker Alice are accompanied by an iconic photo. She's an older lady, with white hair pulled back in a tight bun. Her face is wrinkled and her brow furrowed. And clenched between her teeth is a large, black stogie.

The cigar is as much a part of her legend as the nickname *Poker* in front of Alice. The cigar chomping part of her story is confirmed by her own words as well as reports of people who knew her well. A reporter from *The Plain Dealer* wrote this in 1929:

> Alice smokes big cigars, reads without glasses and addresses her cat in phrases of contented profanity. "I took to cigars down in Mexico City," she explained. "They didn't smoke cigarets much down in old Mexico in those days, and when I was dealing faro I didn't have time to fool with a cigaret."[8]

Beyond Deadwood and Lead

In the mid-1890s, with Warren by her side, Alice traveled a wider circle, well beyond the towns she had known so well in the Colorado Rockies or the confines of Deadwood and Lead. In interviews she mentioned travels as far south as El Paso, Texas, and through southern New Mexico, then west to Clifton, Arizona. That's where she gained one of the worst nicknames in the history of gambling, as she explains:

On one occasion I had brought back a new corduroy suit to
the little camp of Clifton, Arizona. On the first night of my
return I wore it and it seemed that I couldn't lose.

"'I'm glad you didn't buy two of those corduroy suits,"
said a miner as I took a third consecutive pot. "You'd have
broken everybody in the gulch!"

With that I became Corduroy Tubbs, and Corduroy I
remained until my passion for poker brought me a new
and more appropriate name.[9]

Who knows how long she was Corduroy Tubbs? Some stories
imply that Alice didn't become Poker Alice until after Warren's death.

The route north of Arizona and west of South Dakota could
have brought Alice and Warren to camp out among the soothing
hot springs of Thermopolis, Wyoming. No doubt they were visiting in the summer of 1900. Their presence was recorded when a
census taker caught up with the elusive couple and captured their
vital statistics for the census records.[10]

In spite of its many hot springs, Thermopolis could be cold
and somewhat inaccessible in the winter as train tracks did not run
all the way to the town. Thermopolis filled with visitors and sup-
pliers during "the season," thanks to the attraction of Hot Springs
State Park, which opened in 1897. The opportunity for gambling
with unskilled tourists with time on their hands would have been a
great lure for Poker Alice and her husband in the warmer months
of 1900.[11]

Warren G. Tubbs's birthdate—found in the 1900 U.S. Federal
Census—was incorrectly listed as Dec. 1857, instead of 1859. He
and Alice gave their marriage year as 1896. Her age is listed as 31.
Was that a misprint, handwritten by a careless census taker? Or did
she lie about her age to her younger husband? Years spent indoors
and out of the sun may have preserved her complexion, and years
of a practiced poker face may have prevented many lines forming

to reveal her true age. It's a good bet she did lie about her age and not for the first time. In later newspaper articles, when she was proud to have lived as long as she did, she was more likely to tell the truth.

Traveling the West with Warren would have offered a measure of safety Alice didn't enjoy in earlier years. Still, Alice was armed and ready for danger. She made it clear that her skill with a gun allowed her to feel confident whether or not she had a man by her side:

> During many years in some of the roughest, wildest camps of the West, I had cause to draw my gun only twice. Later in life I had occasion to shoot a repeating rifle with rather deadly effect, but that was after my professional gambling days were over. In the older times, my .38 hung year after year in its holster, undisturbed save for the times when it would be brought forth for cleaning and oiling. But it did bark once. A gamester attacked my husband with a knife, disregarding the fact that my gun hand was moving toward the holster. I shot him in his knife arm; that ended the quarrel.[12]

Her .38 came in handy when dealing with a cheating gambler too. It happened during a faro game in which Alice was a player, not the dealer:

> Luck, as I thought, had been running against me. I lost $500, then $1000. When I began on the second $1000 my eyes fastened themselves much harder on the faro box than on the play itself. There seemed something uncanny about the way I was losing. At last I thought I detected a little movement in that box and a thickness about the turn. I watched more closely—for $800 worth, in fact. Then I drew my revolver.
>
> "'If you'd done that cleverly," I said, "there wouldn't have been any kick. I could admire a clever crook, I'll admit that.

This bird's-eye view of Deadwood shows that it lies in a valley surrounded by steep hill-sides. It was an easy journey by train when Alice arrived there in the 1890s. *South Dakota State Historical Society, South Dakota Digital Archives (2009-01-28-008]*

But a clumsy one like yourself — Now before I pull this trigger, you give me back my money!"

When I walked out of that gambling hall I had my $1800, but not my equanimity.[13]

Sometime after the turn of the century, Alice and Warren bought a ranch property and moved there from Lead (a town just four miles from Deadwood). At the decade's start, she was 47, and he was 41. Visits to towns like Thermopolis would have made an interesting break in an otherwise quiet routine. The decade between 1900 and 1910 was a quiet one for Alice and Warren, though the season would end suddenly and sadly on the eve of 1910.

CHAPTER 6

The Black Hills and Beyond

Crooks caused the death of gambling,
just as crooks caused the death of the saloon.

POKER ALICE TUBBS, *The Saturday Evening Post*

W HAT WAS IT LIKE FOR A WOMAN of Alice's adventurous
nature to settle down on a small homestead, several days'
journey from any sizable town? You might think she found it bor-
ing, being isolated and tied to the land. But she later told a friend,
"It was the happiest part of my life." [1]

Where, exactly, was this homestead located? Reports differ.
Some—starting with columnist Warren Morrell in 1949—have stated
it was 48 miles west of Sturgis. That puts the ranch in Wyoming,
near the town of Sundance on the edge of the Black Hills. But Alice's
friend, Kate Soldat, said the ranch was located on the Moreau River,
100 miles north of Sturgis. That location would be consistent with
land rushes that occurred around 1907 in Perkins County, South
Dakota. It means Alice and her husband had at least three happy
years working on their place in the country.

And what about children? Did she and Warren have any
together? Did she ever actually have seven children: four boys and
three girls? That's what many books and newspaper articles written
about her claimed.[2] But the matter of children for Alice remains
unclear for now.

If Alice and Warren Tubbs got together after she left Creede in
1892, Alice would have been about 40 years old when they married

(though she told Warren she was much younger). The 1900 census lists the couple, but no children with them. Possibly they were on a vacation trip (they were staying in a tent, after all), but it's doubtful they would have left seven youngsters back on the ranch while Alice and Warren visited Thermopolis, some 300 rugged miles away.

The notion of Alice and Warren having seven children could have stemmed from a misprint. Newspapers frequently picked up and reprinted articles, often cutting and editing them to fit the available column inches. Fact-checking was not a high priority. One article stated Poker Alice and her husband had *several* children. A single typographic error might have started the tale.

What about the son she mentioned to a reporter, the one who served with the Canadians in World War I, returning as a major?[3] Was he the one she referred to in the 1927 *Saturday Evening Post* article? She said, "The other day, I lent a friend $100 to send his wife to the hospital that she might add an heir to the family. As I did so I could not help reflecting upon the change in viewpoint; my son was born on a ranch twenty-five miles from a town and without a doctor. The experience was not a harrowing; I knew a physician was impossible and that ended the matter."[4]

It's interesting that author Nolie Mumey—whose book *Poker Alice* included numerous unattributed quotes from the 1927 *Saturday Evening Post* piece—paraphrased Alice's quote to read, "The other day I loaned a friend $100 so his wife could go to a hospital and have her baby. I could not help but think how things have changed. In my time they had children on ranches without a doctor."[5] Mumey no doubt could do the math and figure out that Alice may have been too old to have children when she married Warren. His extensive book makes no mention of seven children or even a single son.

The son Alice spoke of may have been a stepson from a previous marriage of Warren's—if Warren was widowed or divorced before he met Alice. If that was the case, perhaps Warren's older children lived with them for a time in Sturgis. Kate Soldat said Alice had a daughter who was being raised by relatives back east.

The truth remains a mystery at this writing, though clues exist in Box 73 in Deadwood.

The Mystery in Box 73

Today the city of Deadwood offers casino gambling and a variety of activities for tourists who pour in each year. It proudly displays its Wild West history through excellent museums, a well-maintained cemetery, and the Homestake Adams Research and Cultural Center (HARCC), which provides public access to one of the state's largest collections of Black Hills archival materials.

The staff of the HARCC graciously prepared for my research visit by locating rare copies of newspaper articles and other Poker Alice-related items. I was excited to don white cotton gloves and carefully handle original magazine features and clippings. The collection I accessed there added greatly to the information and photos in this book.

When I checked the database of photos available, I spotted a list of photos which included the following descriptions of four tintypes:

> Little boy in chair 0093.295.001
> Little girl in chair.....0093.294.001
> Young man...............0093.297.001
> Young girl–teens 0093.295.001

Because they were tintypes, the images weren't available digitally, but the curator offered to locate them in the archive collection for me. The wait was lengthy. I could hear whispers as the curator and other staff went back and forth between the large research room and a closed door. At last I was presented with the four tintypes and the explanation that they were held in Box 73, which wasn't in its designated spot on the archive shelf. After some searching, the box was discovered on a desk in the darkened office of an absent staff member, no doubt carefully set aside in preparation for my visit. The tintypes had been in Alice Tubbs' wallet at the time of her death in 1930.

Who were these children? I searched their faces for clues. The little boy and the young man could have been the same person, appearing to be ages 4 and 17. The girl appeared younger than the boy by about a year, and the same was true for the young man and teen girl. They too could have been younger and older versions of the same child. They are nicely dressed and posed in formal settings. All hold the somber expressions typical of tintypes of their era. The younger children have dark hair and eyes, and both look shy. These children could have been related to Alice. Or not. But they clearly were important to her. She had kept these images safe for decades.

The back side of the faded tintypes offered no identification or written notes. These children aren't telling their names—and neither is Alice.

A Time to Look Back

Alice's days of living on an isolated homestead with Warren (and possibly a teenaged son or daughter) would have given her time to reflect on the changes to the world of gambling. An honest player herself, she was angry that greed eventually changed the nature of professional gambling.

At one time, even those in the legal profession felt confident enough to take their chances at faro tables and in poker games. Alice claimed to have seen the gamblers flooding into San Marcial, New Mexico, during the season court was held. Their intent was to play against the "able jurists of the country." She said it was not unusual to see the judge himself playing faro or poker and hoping for a win.

Alice recounted evidence of honorable behavior in those days:

In the Cactus Gambling Hall in El Paso I once saw a famous financier of the West lose $34,000 on what we called in those days a shoot-mouth. In other words, he had brought but little money with him when he entered the place and, losing that, had begun to borrow from the game to make his bets. When he retired from the gambling hall there were no promises, no agreements, no signing of notes or writing of checks. It was an affair of honor; everybody knew that the next morning the colonel would arrive and in courtly fashion hand over to the game keeper $34,000 in bank notes in payment of his honest debts. That was in fair-and-square days.[6]

Even in the good old days, when most gambling was a fair deal, Alice still observed cheaters at work. She told of men with their fingers sandpapered until "the blood all but oozed through the skin." That was to make their fingers sensitive enough to feel marks in the cards, tiny indentations made with pins or needles. Ordinary, rough hands would not detect these marks, but sensitive fingertips could allow a cheater to read the cards.[7]

Honest players like Alice knew the tricks and were more than ready to give up dishonest players. She said,

When gambling was in the open, it was in the main honest; there were too many shrewd men and women looking on who were only too eager to detect fraudulent methods and expose them. It was when gambling went into the rear rooms of the saloons, behind closed doors and with only a few to watch, that it thrived in chicanery. Those were the days, incidentally, when the saloon-keeping participants in such divertissements would lift a drunken man from the floor and, reaching their own hands into the victim's pockets, spill his money upon the bar and shout, 'Come on boys! He's just ordered drinks for the house.'[8]

Once Alice went out of her way to fleece a man she called Sam. This man was an incessant gambler in the Black Hills district who always complained the game was rigged each time he lost money. Of course, this wasn't the case if he happened to win. It bothered Alice, and she finally had the chance to teach the man a lesson.

The fellow was playing poker against Alice and couldn't seem to lose. She said, "By actual count, he beat twenty-seven sets of threes without me ever winning a hand. If I held three kings, then he would have three aces; and if I drew the three highest card in the deck, he would have a small straight to beat it."[9]

"I've got into a square game at last!" her opponent said.

Alice excused herself and fixed up a deck in a back room, deftly switching the cards on her return. She used a swift kick in the shins to warn the player on her right not to cut the deck, then dealt a hand. The betting started, and by the time the game was over, Alice won back every cent the man had previously taken from her.

"Well, Sam," she asked as she chomped her big cigar, "Was that pot crooked?"

Sam replied, "No, Poker. I guess you've got a right to win a hand once in a while."

She kept the money after failing to convince him the play had not been honest.[10] She stated that was the only time she used a "cold deck," but apparently she could have cheated more often if she wanted to. But where would she have found the thrill in that?

Never on a Sunday

One often-repeated "fact" about Poker Alice is that she was a religious woman, and therefore, she never played poker on Sunday. Was this true? Where does this part of her legend have its roots?

I found no self-reported story or quote where Alice states she refused to play on Sunday, but an article printed nineteen years after her death does make that assertion and adds another story that is often told but has never been verified. In his "Thru the Hills" column in the *Rapid City Journal*, Warren Morrell wrote:

> There was one unusual thing about Poker Alice, some say. She had a religious streak and would not deal on Sunday. Sunday was the big day; the boys came trooping out of the mountains, pouches bearing pay dirt. They were eager to spend it and things worked out exactly right, for the gambling house were willing to take it. But Alice would not deal

on Sunday. The boss of her gambling house said words that never got into any Sunday School leaflet, but she was adamant . . . No Sunday dealing.[11]

Morrell lived in Deadwood and he may have interviewed still-living acquaintances of Alice's to get his information. He also spread a tale that Alice herself never shared in print, that she and Warren were rival faro dealers when they met. "Another table was being operated by a man named W.G. Tubbs. The two were rivals and tried to draw customers from each other. But Alice was young and good looking—poor Tubbs . . . The old, old thing happened. Their rivalry ripened into love and the two were married and moved to a homestead 48 miles west of Sturgis."[12]

A Sad End to a Happy Era

How long did Alice and Warren actually live on their homestead? Accounts differ. It's possible that for some years the couple lived closer to Lead or Sturgis, where the Northwestern Railroad connected regularly with Deadwood. Occasional outings to Deadwood would yield easy winnings for a practiced player like Alice.

That may explain a puzzling 1905 census entry I discovered on the FamilySearch.org website near the end of my research. It reveals that house painter W.G. Tubbs, age 46, was living in Deadwood in 1905. His marital status is marked *single*. Was the couple on a break? Was he really single again? Was Alice at the ranch or off on a gambling adventure? Was it just too difficult for a husband in 1905 to explain his wife's unusual and wandering ways, so he simply told the census taker he was a single man? I opt for the last explanation.

However long the couple's time together lasted as man and wife, the end came at last. The South Dakota Death Index lists the date of Warren's death as December 31, 1909, in Butte County.

According to Alice's old friend of her later years Kate Soldat, "Through his trade as a painter he contracted tuberculosis, and the last years of his life were spent by Alice attempting to regain his

Warren Grant Tubbs is buried in Bear Butte Cemetery in Sturgis, South Dakota. The handsome grave marker is an indication that he was well loved and much missed. *Author's collection*

health. Some months before he died, she moved with him to a ranch on the Moreau River, 100 miles from Sturgis, and there, in a lonely claim shack, Tubbs breathed his last. It was in the dead of winter and the thermometer was registering from 20 to 30 degrees below zero every day." [13]

Warren is buried on a shady hillside in Sturgis' Bear Butte Cemetery, but how he got there is a matter of some question. Like so many accounts surrounding Alice's life, the tale has taken on the quality of legend. One version, first related in Nolie Mumey's *Poker Alice,* has been repeated often as fact, though no primary sources can be found. Still, it's a good read:

> When the snow storm subsided, Alice put the dead frozen body of her husband in a spring wagon and drove forty-eight miles through snowdrifts to get into Sturgis. She had to pawn her wedding ring to obtain enough money for burial expenses. After the services were over, she went into a gambling hall and said, "I want a job of dealing just long enough to earn twenty-five dollars." . . . Once again, with the familiar old black cigar in the corner of her mouth, she matched wits with the best of gamblers . . . When she had earned the specified amount she quit, took the twenty-five dollars, redeemed her ring and returned to her lonely cabin to grieve over her sorrow. [14]

Closing in on her fifty-seventh year, would Alice Tubbs have been able to maneuver the frozen body of her deceased husband into a wagon and drive him either 48 or 100 miles into town for burial? It doesn't sound likely, but it does make a compelling tale.

Still, Kate Soldat backs up the story—positioning the ranch 100 miles from Sturgis. Kate's version includes details that are both plausible and heart wrenching:

> Alice laid him out as best she could, wrapped his body in blankets, put him in a lumber wagon, hitched up the team of horses, and struck across the snow drifted trails to

Sturgis, arriving there towards the close of the fourth day, on a Sunday afternoon.

The last night out the only place she could get to stay was a little dug-out some 25 miles from Sturgis . . . she could have slept on the floor of the dug-out. But with her characteristic faithfulness, she slept not at all, and although it was 25 degrees below zero that night, she spent the night marching around the wagon in which lay the remains of her beloved husband, to protect him from the pack of coyotes that were howling about the place.[15]

What about pawning her ring to pay for the funeral, and earning it back by gambling? She could have easily won the $25 that Mumey's account records. But, according to Kate Soldat, Alice did not pawn her wedding ring, but she did pay $300 for a fine funeral —money she didn't have at the time. (As a comparison, it's verifiable that in 1914, $300 was equivalent to $7,395.72 in 2018.) In debt for the funeral, Alice took a job in Rapid City working for a notorious madam nicknamed Black Nell. Alice's only job at Nell's "resort" was to serve beer to customers. She worked there just long enough to pay back the undertaker for Warren's burial.[16] No doubt she earned enough to pay her debt, but to earn $300 serving beer at Black Nell's would have taken years. Mumey's $25 estimate of the funeral cost must be closer to the actual cost of burying Warren than Kate Soldat's figure of $300.

The year 1910 started a new season in Alice's life, one that would bring her back to the world of poker—and other activities even less socially acceptable. Yet we can understand her need to make money and to take her mind off the pain of a broken heart as she once again grieved the loss of a husband.

This image of Fort Meade and Bear Butte near Sturgis, South Dakota, was used for a post card in 1912. By then, Poker Alice was living in a house within walking distance of Fort Meade. *South Dakota State Historical Society, South Dakota Digital Archives (2008-07-14-006)*

CHAPTER 7

Back in Business

Why do they want me to give up taking a few drinks once in a while?
They might just as well come here and take my cigars away from me,
or [my cat] Calamity Jane, or my memories of the days when they
wouldn't dare to enter my house and search it for liquor.

POKER ALICE, *The Plain Dealer Special*, 1929

WHEN SHE LEFT RAPID CITY, Alice tried to make a go of it in Deadwood once again, but the town had changed during her years away. After decades of notoriety, it was no longer the Wild West. Reformers were up-in-arms about "riff raff" like Alice and determined to rid their town of gambling and prostitution. Though she was known to be an honest player, Alice was lumped in with cheaters and lawbreakers, shunned, and eventually driven out of town.[1]

Resourceful and resilient, Alice packed up and moved to Sturgis, ten miles away. As usual, she gambled and won, raising enough money to buy a small house just outside of town on the north bank of the Bear Butte River. The location was quite strategic.

Alice's new home and place of business, which she called Poker's Palace, was located less than a mile from Fort Meade, a short walk for soldiers on leave. She provided entertainment that included gambling, liquor sales, and eventually, female company at a reasonable price.

According to Kate Soldat, who once served as the mayor of Sturgis, rivalry among the soldiers led to an event Alice would regret the rest of her life.

The South Dakota Militia were in summer training at Fort
Meade, adjoining the city of Sturgis. Poker Alice, her establishment, and the retinue of women that she had with her,
were new to most of the boys who had come from the
prairies of the eastern part of the state. They flocked there
for entertainment and amusement, to the exclusion of the
soldiers of the 12th Cavalry, a squadron of which was sta-
tioned at Ford Meade. Angered at the attention being paid
to what the regular army considered 'tin soldiers,' they
organized a gang and started a raid upon the place.[2]

That Dark Night: July 15, 1913

Poker Alice, Dive Keeper at Sturgis, Kills Soldier,
Wounds Five Others

That was the headline in the local paper on July 16, 1913.[3]
Further details about the deadly incident were sketchy and
contradictory at first.

Two Soldiers Shot During Raid

An attempt was made to raid the place of Alice Tubbs,
north of Sturgis, with the result that Ben Kritzel [sic] of
K troop, First cavalry of Fort Meade was shot and died
about midnight. Joseph C. Minor of the same troop was
also wounded. Mrs. Tubbs, proprietor of the place, and six
inmates are in the county jail here, awaiting developments.
What caused the trouble is not known at this time.[4]

What happened that night? Alice herself said little publicly about
the death of a young man. She did vaguely reference the killing in
one interview. "During many years in some of the roughest, wildest
camps of the West, I had cause to draw my gun only twice. Later in
life I had occasion to shoot a repeating rifle with rather deadly effect,
but that was after my professional gambling days were over."[5]

Eyewitness accounts from the formal investigation and
newspaper articles differ, but Kate Soldat's summary of events

is confirmed by testimony given during the hearing, which exonerated Alice.

> Simultaneously, the telephone and electric light wires were cut on the roof of the building and an assault made on the place. Alice came to the defense of her property. A shot rang out in the midnight air, and one of the regular army men lay dead, others were wounded.[6]

The man who died was Private Ben Koetzle. He had gotten into trouble four years earlier when he deserted only four months after enlisting in the cavalry. He was apprehended in New York, probably headed home to Buffalo, and was eventually returned to duty after paying for the cost of his arrest and transportation.[7]

In spite of this incident, Koetzle wasn't considered a troublemaker the night of the shootings. Soldiers who were there testified that the young man happened to be in the wrong place at the wrong time. Apparently Koetzle was sober when he was last seen alive, and he was just one of some 60 men who converged on Alice's place July 15. He was, however, absent without a pass at the time of his death.[8]

When the lights went out and a mob of soldiers started smashing her windows, Alice fired her rifle in self-defense. Officials agreed that she had the right to take deadly action under the circumstances. The local newspaper reported the conclusion of the affair this way:

No Complaint Filed against Woman Who Killed a Soldier at Sturgis

No complaint has been or will be filed by State's Attorney Gray of Meade county, against Poker Alice Tubbs, who on Monday night last, in her resort at Sturgis shot and killed Private Fred Koestle [sic] a member of the twelfth United States cavalry. A careful and thorough investigation of the facts attending the shooting made by the state's attorney led to the absolute conviction that the woman was justified in the shooting; that at the time she shoot Koestle, [sic] he and other cavalrymen and members of the state militia, now camped at Fort Meade, were engaged in attempting to destroy her personal property and that she was justified in using the means she employed in defending the property.[9]

Though the charges of murder and manslaughter were dropped, Alice wasn't completely off the hook. She was charged with "keeping a house of ill fame," and arrested. She waived examination and was bound over to the circuit court, awaiting trial. Bail was set at $1,000. She was unable to pay it, so she was thrown in jail for a short time. Credible accounts report that she asked for a Bible, and when the sheriff said the jail didn't have one, she sent home for hers. She spent her time reading Scripture and smoking her beloved cigars.[10]

Alice entered a plea of guilty, but the sentencing was postponed and never passed. No judgment was ever entered on her plea.

Meanwhile, the six women "residents" from her house were convicted of frequenting a house of ill fame and fined $15 each.

When the air cleared, business resumed at the little house near the river. But Alice's friends said she was never the same after that tumultuous night of July 15, 1913. Certainly the cloud of murder hung over her head in the years that followed, further tarnishing the reputation of this once polished and proud woman.

Possibly it was all the negative gossip and newspaper accounts that led her to change her name when she remarried in 1918. Could it be that the man who loved her had no idea about the dark past that "Eva" Tubbs may have temporarily buried?

Married for the Third Time

Stories abound regarding Alice's marriage to George Huckert, which official documents record as taking place on December 23, 1918, in Lawrence County, South Dakota. Alice was 65 years of age, but interestingly, her age in the marriage record is given as 52. Her name was listed as Eva Tubbs.

George was 63 at the time of the marriage, so perhaps his eyesight was fading. Or it's possible even the hard times following Warren's death hadn't left many marks of age on the third-time bride.

Multiple features about Alice's colorful life on websites, in newspapers and local history booklets tell the same story about her choice to marry George. The story likely originated in Nolie Mumey's book, where the author attributed it to an unpublished manuscript sent to historian Fred Mazzulla by someone who knew Alice personally:

> A few years after Tubbs died, Poker Alice owned a place quite a few miles from the city of Sturgis where she was raising sheep. She hired Huckert to live on this ranch and raise sheep for her; he came to town every so many months for supplies and she would give him what money he asked for. In the meantime, he fell in love with her and asked her time and time again to marry him, but she always said, "No," she didn't want to marry again. This went on for several years. One day Poker got to thinking she had not paid Mr. Huckert his regular wages for some time so she sat down and figured up what she owed him. She said, "You know I owed him $1008.00 and all I had was about fifty dollars on hand, so I got to figuring it would be cheaper to marry him than to pay him off." Then she laughed heartily at the way she married Mr. Huckert. She felt badly, though, over his death.[11]

This tale is not recounted by Alice herself in any interviews or other first-person quotations. And while many articles state that Huckert died shortly after their marriage, he actually died October 12, 1924, so they had 7 years together, blissful or not. Census records show that George was living in Perkins County, South Dakota, in the Vrooman Township in 1920. He was born in France but spoke German. His occupation was given as hired man/shepherd. His location in Perkins County supports the assertion that Alice's ranch was there, north of Sturgis on the Moreau River.

Meanwhile, the 1920 federal census places Eva E. Huckert in Sturgis, living on Jackson Street. The census also states she was

The original home of Poker Alice was moved to its present location, 1802 South Junction in Sturgis, and carefully restored by the owner. *Author's collection*

born in 1866 (matching the 13 years she deducted from her age when she married George and confirming that Alice was good at arithmetic—especially subtraction when it came to her age). George too is listed as living at the Jackson Street address, but since he was also counted in Perkins County, he may have spent most of his time tending sheep on the remote ranch. However, at the time of his death, he was back in Sturgis.

In spite of marrying for a third time, Alice said she was really in love with Warren Tubbs and that he was the only man she ever loved.[12] She again used the last name of Tubbs after Huckert died, and that is the name engraved on her tombstone in Sturgis' St. Aloysius Cemetery.

Reformed at Last? Not Likely

When the Prohibition Era started in 1920, it seemed possible that Alice might just have to reform her ways. The sale of alcohol was made illegal, and that was a big part of the business at Poker's

Palace. It's true Alice had to cease and desist her public sales, but private use was another matter.

Kate Soldat has this to say, "After prohibition came, Alice discontinued the running of a resort, but continued to live in the same house where she had been making her living. She could never accustom herself to prohibition, or the enforcement of the law, and a few years later, while she and some of her friends were celebrating and were more or less inebriated, officers of the sheriff's office raided her place, and she was arrested."[13]

This new brush with the law took place in 1928, four years after Huckert's death. By this time, Alice was something of a local celebrity, having made headlines, in a positive way, after attracting the attention of national news writers starting in late 1926. Yes, she had finally settled down, but she was not actually reformed. She drank to excess from time to time, as a way to lift her spirits and escape the feelings that must have accompanied days filled with deprivation and poverty.

After her arrest, Alice pled guilty to drunkenness and served 30 days in jail. Then a new State's Attorney took office and decided to bring up an old case against her, convicting her of running a house of prostitution. Though that case was appealed, the judgment was affirmed, and Alice was sentenced to serve six months in the state penitentiary.

Because she had lived so many years in the Black Hills (and had recently received so much good press), Alice found her cause taken up by a group of prominent citizens. They signed an application for the governor to pardon this poor, helpless, elderly lady. For that to happen, she had to travel to Pierre, to meet with South Dakota Governor William J. Bulow for a hearing.

Alice was driven from Sturgis to Pierre by her old friend Kate. The story of their adventures (from the *Rapid City Journal,* June 21, 1953) is too lively to resist including at length:

> Shortly after leaving Sturgis [Alice] twisted and was so uncomfortable that I finally asked, "Is there something

In 1928 Poker Alice Tubbs received a pardon from Governor Bulow after she was sentenced to serve time for dealing in illicit whiskey. Attorney Harry Atwater is shown presenting the pardon to her in Sturgis. *South Dakota State Historical Society, South Dakota Digital Archives (2008-07-07-033)*

wrong?" She replied, "No." Finally, she opened up her blouse and there around her neck, hanging on a small rope or twine, was a hot water bottle in which she was carrying her "little smile," as she called her "nip."

Near the town of Midland, the brakes on my car caught fire. I had difficulty in getting Alice to leave the car. She said, "Honey, there's no use—I might as well burn in the car—that outfit is going to burn me anyway; might as well get it over with."

She created a definite stir at the St. Charles Hotel where she demanded every conceivable attention . . . It was a tussle getting her sobered up before the eventful morning, and instead of driving her to the Capitol, we walked.

Upon seeing the Governor, her first remarks were, "Well, Governor, I have waited a long time to see you; I want you to know that I voted for you. I hope you will turn me loose, so I can go back to my beautiful calico cat." She bantered back and forth to the very apparent amusement of His Honor.[14]

After the hearing, the governor granted a pardon to Poker Alice, citing her advanced years and that she was apparently approaching life's end as his reason. He reportedly said, "I can't send a white-haired old woman to jail on a liquor charge."[15]

Alice was free to return to her little house in Sturgis, where she spent most of her time reading and raising chickens and calico cats. Some neighbors and townspeople saw her wandering around the gentle hills nearby. While she claimed she was hunting wildflowers, friends knew she was more likely hunting for food, which her shooting abilities provided in the form of rabbits and squirrels. Alice herself said, "In childhood I had been able to knock a squirrel from a tree at will. Even today, though my eyes are dimmed for reading, I can still see a target perfectly, and the autumn hunting season finds me invariably in the field."[16]

In spite of her poverty, she gave back to the friends who helped her. These included Kate Soldat, who often ran errands for her and helped with correspondence. "[Alice] had a brilliant mind and corresponded with a lot of big-wigs. She was wonderful at dictating but she never had any money and I never expected any for my work. However, she would frequently reward me with a big kettle of homemade beans, soup or a pie."[17]

Though Alice's life was generally quiet during her later years, it was punctuated with occasional excitement provided by special invitations, travel, and unusual visitors. By 1927, inquisitive reporters at last discovered her colorful past and shared it with a curious nation. Poker Alice was now a household name.

CHAPTER 8

Banking on Fame

I'm supposed to reform now, so they say . . . In fact, I guess I told them I would, but I just can't see how I can. I've been a good woman all my life, so why change now when I'm 76 years old?

POKER ALICE, *The Plain Dealer Special*

A LICE TUBBS WAS AT HOME IN STURGIS when the 1925 South Dakota State Census worker caught up with her. Her answers differ from those of previous years—which either says something important about Alice during this season of her life—namely, that she'd given up lying about her age and was now proud of it. Or it might just throw doubt on the accuracy of the harried census workers. Whichever is true, here are Alice's answers about her own status in 1925:

NAME:	Alice Tubbs
AGE:	72
GENDER:	Female
RACE:	White
BIRTH YEAR:	1853
BIRTH PLACE:	Ohio
ETHNICITY:	Irish
MARITAL STATUS:	Widowed
Marriage Date:	1870
RELIGION:	Baptist
FATHER BIRTH PLACE:	Ireland
MOTHER BIRTH PLACE:	Ireland

Draw your own conclusions about Alice's religious leanings. Though later she would return to the Catholic Church, Alice reported she was attending a Baptist church at the time of the 1925 census. Or perhaps she wasn't going to any church at the time, but Baptist Church members were providing her with needed help, so she said "Baptist."

Her marriage date is listed as 1870. That is possibly the year of her first marriage; she would have been 17 years old when she married Frank Duffield. Why would she give that date and not the date of her marriage to Warren? A marriage certificate has never been found to verify the date Alice married Warren. His obituary stated he married Alice in 1892. The couple told a 1900 U.S. Census taker that they had been married for 4 years. It's entirely possible they met in 1892 and became a married couple through the tradition of common-law marriage. This wasn't unusual, and common-law marriage was recognized as legal marriage in South Dakota until 1959.

Do Alice's 1925 answers about her place of birth and parents' birthplaces shed any more light on her origins? Was she born in Ohio or Virginia? Was her birth year actually 1853, even though her tombstone says 1851? This author's search for documentation continues. There are so many conflicting reports because Poker Alice was about to gain a level of fame few ordinary people would achieve in a pre-television, pre-Internet world.

The Press Discovers Poker Alice

After the undesirable coverage of Alice's self-defense killing of a Fort Meade soldier in 1913, she may have been wary of reporters. Yet some event triggered a story, which led to more stories, which led to national exposure for the former lady gambler. Could that event have been the 1925 Days of '76 celebration in Deadwood, South Dakota?

The first Days of '76 Parade was held in Deadwood in the summer of 1924, 48 years after the legendary times of Wild Bill Hickok and Calamity Jane. The annual celebration included the

This photo was staged for a newspaper article in the 1920s. It features Poker Alice dealing, wearing her usual campaign hat and with a cigar between her teeth. Others are iden-
tified as Fats Schielle, Bill Trathan, Banks Steward, Grasshopper Jim, Howard Landers,
and Fred Borsch. Note the drawn pistol on the left and the photographs of Wild Bill
Hickok and Calamity Jane on the wall. *South Dakota State Historical Society, South
Dakota Digital Archives (2008—07-07-035)*

few old-timers who were left to tell the stories of the Wild West.
Deadwood Dick was one of them, and according to a July 29,
1925, report in the *Huron Evening Huronite,* his appearance
was positively anticipated.

Deadwood Dick to Revive Days of Gold Rush

Richard Clark, the original "Deadwood Dick" of song and
story will take part in the Days of '76 celebration near here
August 12, 13 and 14 if his health permits. Dick is now well
on in years and runs a ranch near Dumont. Recently he
came to Deadwood to have an injured arm treated.

Deadwood Dick likes to joke about the character he has been painted in the story books. As a matter of fact he is credited with being a very gentle and kindly man.[1]

As Alice likely knew Deadwood Dick from her days in Deadwood and Lead, she may have decided to get in on the action. It's unknown who alerted the media, but on March 24, 1926, an article was published in the *Sioux City Journal* describing "one of the best known characters of the early days of the Black Hills . . . one that history has overlooked." The reporter, a columnist called Sunshine Sinie, wisely noted that Poker Alice was different from headline-grabbers like Calamity Jane:

> She was known at every card table throughout the Black Hills, but unlike Calamity Jane, she depended not on a reputation given her by newspaper and magazine writers, but on one she had earned for herself by being able to take her share of the money away when the game ended.
>
> Her name never occupied a place in the headlines nor did she thrill the pioneers with her 'quick draw' and sudden shooting. She just went along tending to her own business, playing the game without publicity, mixing with the wild men and women and their lives without ostentation or show, but playing a good game of poker and getting her share of the money that was being thrown away by miners just in from a lucky strike.[2]

Alice's quiet life in the shadows came into the light. She was interviewed for *The Saturday Evening Post* by renowned reporter Courtney Ryley Cooper. The article, entitled "Easy Come, Easy Go," appeared in the national publication on December 3, 1927. It was extensive and compelling—an "as-told-to" piece that captured Alice's unique voice. It inspired many other reporters to revise it for their own papers or interview her on their own. It also formed the foundation for books and articles that would be written many decades later. Multiple stories and quotes included this book came from Cooper's thorough and thrilling article.

Alice's later years were filled with excitement and new adventures, thanks to the exposure she gained nationally. Of course, her new fame meant that Governor Bulow's pardon in 1928 would trigger even more coverage, especially throughout 1929.

A reporter named Earl B. Douglas found a photo of younger Alice to run next the famous image of white-haired Alice with her big black cigar. Much of his article, which was reprinted extensively, seems to be an imaginative rewrite of Cooper's facts, but it does include some new information.

> Poker Alice was born Alice Ivers in Sudburg, [sic],
> Devonshire, England in 1853. When she was three her
> parents brought her to America. The family settled in the
> south, where she was graduated from a woman's college.
> During the Civil war, her father was a colonel in the
> Confederate army, commanding the Nineteenth Louisiana
> infantry. Two of her brothers were killed in the battle of
> Malvern hill.[3]

Unfortunately, this article introduces some inaccurate information that was picked up and widely distributed as fact. First, her birthplace, Sudbury, is misspelled *Sudburg*. Second, although the author states that Alice arrived in Deadwood "just in time for the killing and burial of 'Wild Bill'" in 1876, there is no evidence for such an early arrival by Alice.

Douglas did get one thing right: "Because of her 'poker' face, she won the sobriquet which she ever since has carried."[4]

A colorfully written article appeared in the *Defiance Crescent News* on April 1, 1929. It was quickly picked up by papers across the nation, possibly due to the eye-catching photo of Alice and the headline, "75 Year-Old 'Poker Alice' Craves Her Stogie." Unfortunately, this article introduced more unverified, unlikely information that soon was shared as gospel truth:

> At 38, she married W.G. Tubbs and bore him seven
> children. Two survive, a splendid son and pre-possessing

daughter . . . A fortune teller once told Alice she would live 100 years. And Alice certainly bids fair to fulfilling that prediction. At 75 she still reads without glasses, as the photo shows, and comes out of a three-day 'binge' without so much as a sign of indigestion, or a blemish on her face!

The *Oakland Tribune's* May 25, 1929 edition featured a full-page article about Alice, though it appears to have been rewritten from *The Saturday Evening Post* and *Defiance Crescent News* pieces. It references "Sudburg," England. And it mentions the seven children born to Alice and Warren. However, it adds the "fact" that "One of her sons served with the Canadians during the World War and came home a major."

If Alice did have a son, or helped raise a son of Warren's, it would be consistent with the tintype of the young man found with her belongings after her death. He could have been eighteen at the time of the Great War and may have, indeed, fought with the Canadians.

Alice's Adventures in Chicago and Omaha

With access to the railroad and willing sponsors, Alice found herself traveling once again. In October 1929, she made a special journey:

> Poker Alice Tubbs, who used to deal faro in mining camp gambling houses and still enjoys a good cigar, started for Chicago today to see the world series.
>
> "Most women of my age . . . would probably be packing up to attend some civic club meeting, but not for mine. I'm going to Chicago and I want to see them Chicago Cubs win the pennant."
>
> Poker Alice also is an ardent fan and seldom misses a good card staged in the Black Hills."[5]

Let us hope Alice chose not to bet money on her team as the Cubs lost the 1929 series in five games to the Philadelphia Athletics.

The most recognizable image of Poker Alice Tubbs appeared in newspapers across the United States in the late 1920s and was featured on many postcards. *Courtesy Deadwood History, Inc., Adams Museum Collection, Deadwood, SD*

A month later, Alice traveled to Omaha, Nebraska, to help celebrate the state's Diamond Jubilee—the 75th anniversary of Nebraska's incorporation as a territory. She and Deadwood Dick were featured at the head of the parade, wearing costumes from days gone by. Alice's normal garb, a dark brown suit, man's gray shirt, and regulation Army cavalry hat made her a picturesque sight to the crowds and reporters at the parade.

A poker game was staged, including Alice, Deadwood Dick, and a few other old timers. She took the challenge seriously, even demanding that a noisy radio be turned down so she could concentrate. "How can anybody draw cards with that going on?" she asked. After winning the hand with a low straight, she still complained as she scooped up her chips, "That darned radio pretty near made me draw wrong."[6]

And There Is a Night in Creede

Her newfound fame enabled Alice to at last tell her stories and redeem some of the difficult times she'd faced in the years after Warren died. The publicity led old friends and acquaintances to seek her out and relive memories of the old days.

Imagine how it felt for Alice, long gone from the lively mining towns she knew so well, to hear how they fared more than thirty years later. Some were going strong, but others were in steep decline. Some were complete ghost towns. She told a reporter:

> I met a friend not long since who had been to both Creede and Bachelor. There was no main street any more in the latter town; only a collection of tumble-down buildings with the roofs fallen in, the walls awry and the wooden sidewalks rotted back to the earth. The gambling halls where I worked, and a play of $25,000 or $30,000 a night was not at all unusual, are merely piles of rotten boards now.
>
> In all the town during my friend's visit, only one spiral of smoke came from a chimney and that was not due to a permanent resident. A sheep herd was passing through

By 1922, the once thriving town of Bachelor, Colorado, had few residents and many abandoned buildings. Without the high-mountain setting, Alice would not have recognized it. *Courtesy of the Creede Historical Society*

on the way to higher country and a summer's grazing. The herd crew had selected one house of the town which seemed habitable and decided to pass the night there. As for Creede, there had not been even a restaurant open at 8:30 o'clock at night; only a few street lights glimmering and perhaps a dozen men on the street. And this was the town where there had been no night, whatever and where the trains, arriving as fast as the motive power would permit, carried such crowds that men even rode on the tops of the passenger cars![7]

It's a wonderful thing that the media discovered Alice, even so late in her life. The vivid memories she shared with eager listeners and reporters continue to bring the past to life—even to the present day.

Poker Alice's gravesite in the St. Aloysius Cemetery in Sturgis is visited often by those who have heard her story and appreciate her legacy. *Author's collection*

CHAPTER 9

Cashing in Her Chips

I suppose I should enjoy knitting. But I would rather sit in a game with four or five expert poker players than eat, and though it may sound egotistic, I have never found anyone yet who grew humpbacked carrying away the money he won from me.

POKER ALICE, *The Saturday Evening Post*

A FTER A LIFETIME OF GAMBLING, Poker Alice was used to taking a risk, betting it all, and winning. But in 1930, she rolled the dice one last time. The stakes were the highest: life or death.

After the previous year's media attention and excitement, Alice may have felt new energy and determination to live her last years to the fullest. But her health was getting in the way. She suffered from gallstones that caused intense pain, to a point where death didn't look so bad, according to her friend Kate Soldat, who was interviewed by the *Rapid City Journal*:

> She frequently told her friends that she would welcome death as the end of her terrible sufferings. However, three weeks before her death, doctors had convinced her that there was some chance for her recovery, through an operation, but the chance was small. Life had been one long game of chance for Poker Alice. Nerve was her long suit; fear was an element that knew no place in her character.[1]

Feisty Alice refused to use a wheelchair after she entered St. John's Hospital in Rapid City, South Dakota. Though her nurses insisted, she said she preferred to walk. She only relented when the Mother Superior appealed to her practical side, "Alice, you want to get your money's worth, don't you?"

As she entered the operating room, Alice was reported to be calm and confident, bantering with her nurses and teasing her handsome surgeon, Dr. Doyle. She survived the surgery but remained in the hospital for three weeks due to serious complications. She lost her final bet and died there on February 27, 1930.

Alice had prepared to meet her Maker. Her will was updated and clear. She gave her wedding ring—a plain, gold band—to her dear friend Kate. And before death took her, she received the last rites of the Catholic Church.

Friends and acquaintances attended her funeral Mass and listened to a short sermon by the Rev. Father Columban. He told the biblical story of the woman caught in adultery. Dragged before Jesus Christ by the Pharisees, facing death for her sins, she was set free by these words of grace, "Let him who is without sin cast the first stone." The *Rapid City Journal* summarized the services:

> Throughout his sermon there ran constantly his theme "God's Mercy Endureth Forever," and the many old timers who knew Poker Alice throughout her stormy career joined in the prayer that may "God's mercy endure for her." [2]

Alice was buried in St. Aloysius Cemetery in Sturgis on a peaceful hillside next to the church. Visiting her grave, I was surprised to see a simple gift of three silk flowers that someone left at her headstone. Were they placed in remembrance by a distant relative, or even a descendant? Or were they left by another fan who admired one-of-a-kind Alice? Her gravesite attracts visitors throughout the year.

Sadly, it appears her relatives were not there for her in her old age. So she cut them out of her will. The document states: "I hereby specifically disinherit each and every one of my relatives and kin, for the reason that they have not contributed to my welfare and happiness during the declining years of my life, nor have they made any effort to inquire as to my welfare for a great number of years."[3]

Flowers at her grave in Sturgis are one affirmation that Alice is not forgotten, though the straight story of her adventures became terribly tangled in the fiction that followed after her death.

Sorting Fact from Fiction

The day after her death, newspapers across the nation published Alice's obituary. One widely distributed feature ran in the *Helena Daily Independent* on February 28, 1930. Only partly accurate, it displays the hyperbolic language typical in newspapers of the day, and offers exaggerations often found in articles about Poker Alice:

> "Poker Alice" Tubbs, 77, picturesque character of the Old West where she was a fixture in the mining camps of the gold rush era, coppered her last bet today and lost. Ironic was the fate which permitted her to come unhurt through numerous gambling gun fights to die after an operation.
>
> From the Pecos to the Colorado through gold fields, Tonopah and Butte, "Poker Alice," in the 80's dealt her cards. Faro here, chuck-a-luck there, and now and then a bit of craps, they were all the same to the girl.
>
> An associate of the "big shots" of border days, Alice numbered among her acquaintances "Wild Bill" Hickok, "Calamity Jane," "Deadwood Dick," "Tex" Rickard and others who took their whisky neat, their cards high.
>
> As she was deft at dealing cards, so was she equally agile at handling the six-gun, the only law recognized in the hectic days of Tombstone, Carson City, Dodge City and on the Brazos. . . . One after another they died, some in their boots, others in a lone prospector's camp, under the Colorado skies, or a crawling, choking death on the alkaline Nevada Desert. . . .
>
> Today, she died, and another page in the book of western lore was turned.

In addition to newspaper articles that cropped up after her death, Alice was mentioned in early books about the Wild West, including *Calamity Jane and the Lady Wildcats* by Duncan Aikman published during her life in 1927.

Seizing an opportunity to fill the need for book about Alice's life, historian Nolie Mumey produced a limited edition of 500 numbered and signed copies of *Poker Alice* in 1951. While Mumey's book contains portions from unpublished manuscripts, as well as Alice's last will and testament, much of the book is based on the 1927 *Saturday Evening Post* article by Courtney Ryley Cooper. It lacks dates and details, as well as any bibliography or sources.

A one-page profile about Poker Alice can be found in *Outlaw Album* by Fred and Jo Mazzulla (published by the H. B. Hirschfeld Press in 1966). It lists her birth year as 1851 and asserts "A college graduate, she taught school in Lake City, Colorado, and married Duffield, a mining engineer, there in 1873." Since Lake City was incorporated in 1873, this is a possibility, but the date of the couple's marriage has yet to be verified by any credible source.

Mildred Fielder's story of Poker Alice was first published in 1969 under the title *Deadwood's Lady of Cards*. A later booklet by the same author and published in 1978 is filled with unique photographs and contains a helpful bibliography. Fielder, along with other writers, believes that Alice and her husband went to Deadwood for the 1876 gold rush. That theory doesn't line up with Alice's own stories, or with the date Warren gave for their marriage, which was 1892.

Alice did state that she had known Calamity Jane, who was in Deadwood in 1876. But it makes more sense that the two well-known western women met in Deadwood when Calamity Jane returned there in the mid-1890s.

With so many tales floating around about Alice's early years, it seems natural that her story would attract fiction writers such as John Jakes, who based his 1980 short story, "The Winning of Poker Alice," on a "meet cute" with Warren Tubbs. His story embellished the story of Alice saving Warren's life from a knife-welding gambler with a well-placed shot.

And, of course, Hollywood couldn't resist creating its own version of Alice's adventures.

The made-for-television movie called *Poker Alice* released in 1987 starred Elizabeth Taylor as Alice and George Hamilton as her (invented and extremely tan) cousin and traveling companion. The movie is a lively account of the perfectly-coiffed and pastel-suited Alice making her way across the Wild West. It doesn't have much to do with the real Poker Alice, but Elizabeth Taylor looks beautiful in the film, and it's worth watching for a few laughs and light-hearted entertainment—not to mention that really big 1980s hair.

Until the Internet came into being, most reports about Alice over the years were found in newspapers such as the *Denver Post,* usually in stories covering a variety of wilder women of the West. Most of these articles appear to be based on earlier stories, so the same mistakes were handed down and questionable legends were built up.

Today trying to sort the truth from all the myths online is a hefty challenge. When it comes to researching facts on the Web, it's the Wild West all over again. Alice's ghost could not be very pleased. In fact, she's knocked me in the head a few times for some performances re-enacting her life in which I too spread untrue tales before I discovered how many of them canceled out each other!

A House on the Move

Given that nomadic Alice didn't settle down for many years, it's no surprise that her home in Sturgis also moved around a bit. It was in two different locations before it landed at its current spot at the intersection of Junction Avenue and Deadwood Street.

This final chapter in Alice's story started with a headline in the *Rapid City Journal,* October 23, 1974.

Bawdy House to Be a Museum?

Sturgis—Plans for preservation of a house of ill repute as a museum or showplace in a Bear Butte Creek Park are in the mill at Sturgis.

It is the former home of a woman who a little more than a year before her death was pardoned by Gov. William J. Bulow after being convicted for maintaining just such a house.[4]

The house started out on the south side of Bear Butte Creek, on Jackson Street as listed in the 1920 Census. A log bridge connected the residence to the main part of town. In her will, Alice left the house to her friend, Kate Soldat, along with a $700 mortgage to pay off. Kate eventually gave it to Mrs. Harriet Wilmer, who could keep up with the mortgage payments. It was later sold to Chris Sorenson.

In 1972, a major flood damaged the property and threatened the foundation. So the house was moved to a location on the north side of Bear Butte Creek, at the end of Junction Street. When the Sorenson family moved out, the house fell into disrepair, and was finally bought by the city.

By 1987, the question of whether and how to save the historic, but decaying house was up for debate. The disagreement came to light after a meeting held by the Sturgis Area Chamber of Commerce. Reporter Debra Holland wrote in the *Rapid City Journal:*

"I have a feeling there might have been one or two groups at the meeting that will be going to the council to support saving the structure," said Bob Davis, Sturgis businessman and member of the tourism committee.

Davis said the tourism committee wanted the house saved but wasn't insisting that the committee be the group to do it.

"We do think that it can be moved," Davis said . . . "As far as restoring the building, it's in pretty bad shape.

There's not much there. It's still standing but that's about it. Some people would be happy to have it burned down, but others are interested in preserving that part of history."

Davis said the current controversy arose after nearby residents complained that the building had become an eyesore and threat to public safety.[5]

By 1990, the house would find a savior, but not before a desperate effort to get outside investors to pay for the restoration and relocation. The *Rapid City Journal* noted, "The effort included trying to gain the attention of actress Elizabeth Taylor, who was making a television movie in 1987 about Poker Alice. Although Taylor did not step forward, businessmen from Rapid City and the 1880 town near Murdo bid up to $600 for the house."[6]

Finally, the city sold the house to Treat Walker for $1, on his promise to restore it and keep the house in Sturgis. He spent thousands of dollars preserving the home and paid for the 10-block move to its current location. The house was added to the National Register of Historic Places in 1990.

Today the home, painted a bright white with green trim, can be seen sitting on the corner, next to the Junction Inn Motel, at 1802 Junction Street.[7] Like Alice herself, it has found its final resting place, accessible to history and poker fans alike.

TOP: Based on an unverified, but commonly accepted image, this drawing shows Alice (Ivers) Duffield in her early twenties. LEFT: Alice in the 1880s when she was in her thirties, drawn from an unverified photograph said to be of Alice. RIGHT: This portrait is based on a photo of Alice as she appeared in her sixties. The photo was reproduced in many newspapers in the late 1920s. *Portraits by Jeff Barnes, Niddy Griddy Design, Inc. Copyright 2018 by Jeff Barnes. All rights reserved.*

Afterword:
Showing Her Hand

Alice Ivers Duffield Tubbs Huckert. Mrs. Duffield. Corduroy Tubbs.
POKER ALICE.

♠ SHE WAS TRULY AN AMAZING WOMAN. In an era when women were not considered safe and proper unless they stayed home under the protection of a husband or a father, she made her own way. She used her skills to compete with men and to win against all comers, fair and square.

Alice saw a tremendous number of changes in her lifetime. In many ways her story is the story of the Wild West. She experienced firsthand the impact of silver and gold mining on isolated mountain towns. She watched those towns grow, and she lived long enough to learn that some of them had turned to ghost towns. She treasured the vast open spaces of Wyoming and South Dakota. She learned what could happen when reformers wanted to clean up their history, and she was celebrated when that history became fashionable again.

Today, a historical re-enactor rides each year in Deadwood's Days of '76 parade, bringing Poker Alice and her times to life again. Her story lives on, both in myth and in truth.

When I spent some quiet time at her graveside on a warm summer day, I talked to her spirit, her memory, her ghost—whatever you believe lingers there. I promised I'd do my best to track down her true story and share it with people who might find it inspiring in some way.

In her life, Alice was tough. She was tender. She loved and she lost. She hit life's lowest point, and she climbed to a place of redemption. She found hope and forgiveness in her faith.

Poker Alice Tubbs refused to sit on the sidelines. She gambled on life—and won.

Endnotes

CHAPTER 1

1. Courtney Ryley Cooper, "Easy Come, Easy Go," *The Saturday Evening Post*, (Dec. 3, 1927), p. 20. Some books and articles cite Alice's first home and the place where Frank died as Leadville. I have relied on this "as told to" article written by a renowned reporter who interviewed Alice firsthand. It is my main source for quotes and key facts about her life.
2. Ibid.
3. Lambert Florin, *Ghost Towns of the Rockies*, (Superior Publishing Company, 1970), 39-40.
4. Cited in Wikipedia, "Lake City, Colorado," (accessed April 9, 2016). https://en.wikipedia.org/wiki/Lake_City,_Colorado.
5. Cooper, *The Saturday Evening Post*, p. 20.
6. Ibid.
7. Wayne Erbsen, *Manners and Morals of Victorian America* (Asheville, North Carolina, Native Ground Books & Music, 2009), pp. 68, 105, 167.
8. Ibid., p. 90.
9. Cooper, *The Saturday Evening Post*, p. 20.

CHAPTER 2

1. Florin, *Ghost Towns of the Rockies*, p. 13-14.
2. Cooper, *The Saturday Evening Post*, p. 20.
3. Daniel and Beth R. Barrett, *High Drama*, (Montrose, Colorado: Western Reflections Publishing Co., 2005), p. 83-84.
4. Ibid, p. 85.
5. Ibid. p. 90.

6. Cooper, *The Saturday Evening Post*, p. 20.
7. Barrett, *High Drama*, p. 12.
8. Florin, *Ghost Towns of the Rockies*, pp. 15-16.
9. Cooper, *The Saturday Evening Post*, p. 109.
10. Florin, *Ghost Towns of the Rockies*, pp. 31-33.
11. Ibid. p. 58.
12. "A Brief History," www.historictrinidad.com/history.html, accessed January 23, 2017.
13. History: Alamosa County: the first 100 years as told by the sacred mountain of the east, https://alamosacountycentennial.wordpress.com/about, accessed January 23, 2017.
14. History, http://www.delnortecolorado.com/history.html, accessed January 23, 2017.
15. Cooper, *The Saturday Evening Post*, p. 114.

Chapter 3

1. http://www.legendsofamerica.com/ks-caldwell.html.
2. http://www.kansas.com/news/local/news-columns-blogs/the-story-of-kansas/article1113976.html.
3. Cooper, *The Saturday Evening Post*, p. 108.
4. Ibid. p. 21.
5. Ibid. p. 21.
6. Duncan Aikman, *Calamity Jane and the Lady Wildcats*, (New York: Henry Holt, 1927) pp. 310-311.
7. https://www.pagat.com/poker/history.html.
8. https://www.legendsofamerica.com/we-faro.html.
9. Cooper, *The Saturday Evening Post*, p. 113.
10. Ibid. p. 20.

Chapter 4

1. Leland Feitz, *Creede: A Quick History*, (Little London Press: Colorado Springs, Colo., 1969), pp. 7-11.
2. Cooper, *The Saturday Evening Post*, p. 20.
3. Ibid, p. 108.
4. Mrs. A.H. Major, *Colorado History Magazine*, vol. 21, November 1944, p. 216.

5. Cooper, *The Saturday Evening Post,* p. 108.
6. Ibid., p. 109.
7. Ibid., p. 109.
8. Ibid., p. 109.
9. Ibid., p. 113
10. Feitz, p. 25.
11. Kenneth Jessen, *Eccentric Colorado: A Legacy of the Bizarre and Unusual,* (Loveland, Colorado; J.V. Publications, 1985), pp. 100-101.
12. Cooper, *The Saturday Evening Post,* p. 113.
13. Feitz, p. 25.
14. Cooper, *The Saturday Evening Post,* p. 113.
15. From "Creede," a poem by Cy Warman, as reprinted in *Creede.: A Quick History.*

CHAPTER 5

1. The events described in this chapter, based on Alice's *Saturday Evening Post* interview (the most thorough and credible source of information about her life), include mentions of her husband, which supports the timeline presented.
2. Cooper, *The Saturday Evening Post,* p. 21.
3. Ibid., p. 21.
4. Ibid., p. 21.
5. Ibid., p. 21.
6. Ibid., p. 21.
7. Ibid., p. 113.
8. "'Poker Alice,' 76, Still a Bluffer," *Plain Dealer Special,* Feb. 3, 1929.
9. Cooper, *The Saturday Evening Post,* p. 109.
10. The 1900 census lists Warren G. Tubbs, age 42, and his wife, Alice, age 31, as having been married for 4 years. It places them in the town of Thermopolis, Wyoming, living in a tent.
11. Annette Hein, "Hot Springs County, Wyoming," http://www.wyohistory.org/encyclopedia/hot-springs-county-wyoming.
12. Cooper, *The Saturday Evening Post,* p. 106.
13. Ibid.

CHAPTER 6

1. Nolie Mumey, *Poker Alice*, (Artcraft Press: Denver, Colorado, 1951), p. 23.
2. Mildred Fielder, *Poker Alice* (Centennial Distributors: Deadwood, S. Dakota, 1970), p. 13 and the *Defiance Crescent News*, "75-year-old Poker Alice Craves her Stogie," April 1, 1929, p. 1.
3. *Oakland Tribune*, "Poker Alice Tubbs," May 25, 1929.
4. Cooper, *The Saturday Evening Post*, p. 109.
5. Mumey, *Poker Alice*, p. 40.
6. Cooper, *The Saturday Evening Post*, p. 106.
7. Ibid., p. 106.
8. Ibid., p. 106.
9. Ibid., p. 113.
10. Ibid., p. 113.
11. Warren Morrell, "Thru the Hills," *Rapid City Journal*, June 7, 1949, p. 36.
12. Ibid.
13. Kate Soldat, "Poker Alice's Career Had Pathetic, Stormy Events," *Rapid City Journal*, June 21, 1953, p. 6.
14. Mumey, *Poker Alice*, p. 23.
15. Soldat, "Poker Alice's Career Had Pathetic, Stormy Events," p. 7.
16. Ibid.

CHAPTER 7

1. John H. Monnett and Michael McCarthy, *Colorado Profiles*, Niwot, University Press of Colorado, 1996, p. 62.
2. Soldat, "Poker Alice's Career Had Pathetic, Stormy Events" *Rapid City Daily Journal*, June 21, 1953, p. 6.
3. Marian Eatherton, "One Dead, five wounded," *Lawrence County Centennial*, March 30, 2000, pp. 13, 15. Based on research from local historian Bob Lee.
4. *Maryville Daily Democrat Forum*, July 16, 1913, p. 3.
5. Cooper, *The Saturday Evening Post*, p. 106.
6. Soldat, p. 6.
7. Eatherton, p. 13.
8. Eatherton, p. 13.
9. *Huron Weekly State Spirit*, July 24, 1913, p. 7.

10. Mumey, *Poker Alice,* p. 32.
11. Mumey, pp. 29-30.
12. Mumey, p. 30.
13. Soldat, p. 6.
14. Soldat, p. 6.
15. "'Poker Alice' Old West Figure, Died After Operation" *The Helena Daily Independent,* February 28, 1930.
16. Cooper, *The Saturday Evening Post,* p. 20.
17. Kate Soldat, quoted by Lyn Gladstone, "Bawdy house to be museum?" *Rapid City Journal,* October 23, 1974.

CHAPTER 8

1. *Huron Evening Huronite,* July 29, 1925, p. 7.
2. "Poker Alice Played Good Game of Draw," *Sioux City Journal,* March 24, 1926, p. 17.
3. Earl Douglas, "Poker Alice: Pardon Brings Famous Character Peace," *Evening Independent,* February 20, 1929, p. 6.
4. Ibid.
5. "No 'Pink Teas' For 'Poker Alice' Tubbs," *Clovis Evening News Journal,* October 5, 1929, p. 1.
6. "Poker Player Says Radio Ruined Game," *Wisconsin Rapids Daily Journal,* December 7, 1929, p. 11.
7. Cooper, *The Saturday Evening Post,* p. 108.

CHAPTER 9

1. Soldat, *Rapid City Journal,* p. 6.
2. Ibid.
3. Excerpt from Alice Huckert's will, originally published in *Poker Alice* by Mumey.
4. Lyn Gladstone, "Bawdy house to be museum?" *Rapid City Journal,* October 23, 1974.
5. Debra Holland, "Sturgis Debates Saving Historic House," *Rapid City Journal,* January 28, 1987.
6. Pat Dobbs, "Movers move Poker Alice's 'bawdiest of bawdy' house," March 24, 1990, *Rapid City Journal.*
7. Ibid.

Bibliography

Aikman, Duncan. *Calamity Jane and the Lady Wildcats*. New York: Henry Holt, 1927.

Barrett, Daniel and Beth R. Barrett. *High Drama*. Montrose, Colorado: Western Reflections Publishing Co., 2005.

Erbsen, Wayne. *Manners and Morals of Victorian America*. Asheville, North Carolina, Native Ground Books & Music, 2009.

Feitz, Leland. *Creede: A Quick History*. Colorado Springs, Colorado: Little London Press, 1969.

Fielder, Mildred. *Poker Alice*. Deadwood, S. Dakota: Centennial Distributors, 1970.

Florin, Lambert. *Ghost Towns of the Rockies*. New York, New York: Promontory Press, 1987.

Jessen, Kenneth Jessen, Eccentric *Colorado: A Legacy of the Bizarre and Unusual*. Loveland, Colorado: J.V. Publications, 1985.

Mazzulla, Fred and Jo Mazzulla. *Outlaw Album*. Denver, Colorado: A.B. Hirschfeld Press, 1966.

Monnett, John H. and Michael McCarthy, *Colorado Profiles: Men and Women Who Shaped the Centennial State*. Niwot: University Press of Colorado,1996.

Mumey, Nolie. *Poker Alice*. Denver, Colorado: Artcraft Press, 1951.